LET HEALING FLOW, LORD

Let Healing Flow, Lord

Mike Endicott

Terra Nova Publications

Published in Great Britain by
Terra Nova Publications Ltd
PO Box 2400, Bradford on Avon, Wiltshire BA15 2YN

ISBN   1 901949 14 1

Cover design: Gazelle Creative Productions

Printed in Great Britain by Cox & Wyman, Reading

Contents

PROLOGUE

We who know the Father through the grace of Jesus Christ, and have experienced the power of the Holy Spirit, also have the inexpressible privilege of sharing his love and his work for, 'We are therefore Christ's ambassadors, as though God were making his appeal through us' (2 Corinthians 5:20). We have this treasure in 'jars of clay'. We share the glorious good news of salvation, healing and wholeness in Christ because we want all to know 'the peace of God, which transcends all understanding' (Philippians 4:7). In love and compassion, we want to share the knowledge of Christ.

Seen in this 'giving' light, it becomes easier for me to write and speak about the physical, emotional and spiritual blessings of healing prayer—which is at the heart of our ministry at The Well Centre. What we see God doing is not just the fruit of our own prayers, but those of numerous people privately praying for us, too.

To his glory, God has raised up a Centre for prayer and ministry—out of virtually nothing but a derelict church building in South Wales and the faith of four people. These intrepid explorers of God's will have established a Christian Order of healing and wholeness which stretches all over the

United Kingdom and beyond, seeking out those with a calling to the healing ministry, and preparing them under the authority of the Christian Church: an exciting project!

This is the story of the spiritual journey taken by that small group of people, who were stumbling in the half-light of uncertainty until, eventually, the vision became reality.

My special thanks go to Ann Scholey, Jean Hadfield, Sheila Howard and Wyn Herd who, together with Rowan, Archbishop of Wales, have hung on to me through what has sometimes been a bumpy ride.

These days, wherever I turn, I come across people who have been praying for us along the way, mostly without our knowledge. I am immensely grateful to them for their faithfulness. Who knows, this journey might not have been made without them.

1

THE WAY TO THE WELL

To be crucified means, first, the man on the cross is facing only one direction; second, he is not going back; and third, he has no further plans of his own.

A. W. Tozer

I spent the first forty-eight years of my life doing almost exactly the opposite. Far from looking only one way, I searched every avenue for promotion and advancement in life. Even with dimming eyesight, I reached the dizzy heights of being the youngest manager in a huge manufacturing concern. I prided myself on my own strength and courage, which I somewhat foolishly imagined to be the sole source of my success.

As for 'not going back', I found this a constant source of joy. Encroaching blindness left me with only the memories of bygone, youthful days when I was able to do things that a young man can and should do. As my vision failed, the need grew to spend more and more time reflecting on those wonderful times. All the things I had seen and the places I had been to were logged away for safe keeping in the album of memory. All were lovingly re-visited as often as possible.

From God, I only wanted one thing—my physical healing. As my life in manufacturing industry grew more and more difficult to cope with, it seemed that a good, solid piece of eyesight healing intervention from God might allow me to go back to a 'successful' lifestyle.

As for 'having no plans of his own', I had lots of them! With the growing awareness that my deteriorating sight would not sustain me in industrial management for the rest of my working life, I tried all sorts of things. I had a go at pottery, writing and gardening, even toying with the idea of photography and painting. I considered the possibility of becoming a magistrate, and I offered myself for training for ordination in the Anglican Church, as well. All was to no avail. None of these plans came to fruition; not one seemed to satisfy.

Then, the day dawned when I had completely run out of plans. I had very little eyesight left, no career prospects, and memories were fading with the approach of middle-age.

The firm I worked for was cutting back heavily on staff, and my own personal productivity was going downhill as each month passed. My sight began to go more rapidly. I was in trouble and had nowhere to go. My vision of a perfect, ideal life was fading. I ran hard into the brick wall of reality.

However, it is where the ideal meets the real that exploration truly begins. In sheer desperation, I asked Jesus Christ to take over. Having spent most of my life as a church-goer, brought up in the faith, I now became a Christian in the New Testament sense of the word. I became a disciple of the Son of God—a 'student' of the Lord Jesus Christ. There was so much to learn, and so much to un-learn.

There followed a battle of gigantic proportions as I fought to understand how it was that, as the Church had always taught me, God was good and yet, despite the loving prayers and ministry of many friends, my healing never came.

However, God had his own ideas. At the foot of the cross of his Son, he exchanged all my wounds and sore places for his abundant peace. That place has since become a haven for me—somewhere for a wounded soldier to lie down.

Out of my struggle to find a 'good' God came The Well Centre, lovingly nurtured into life by faithful prayer partners; and best described in a local church magazine article:

THE WELL CENTRE is run by a registered charity called the Cwmbran Mission of Christian Healing and takes its spiritual authority through its chaplain, to the Bishop of Monmouth.

The Centre is not a church, but a place where people come to receive the benefits of the Church's ministry of healing and wholeness from a team of highly trained people who minister in quiet love and acceptance.

Most of the work is run on an appointment system and is always private and confidential, offering times of listening, prayer and ministry to those needing God's help in their lives. Those who come are ordinary Christian folk from all walks of life, both lay people and leaders, and the Centre's catchment area is roughly from North Wales to Plymouth, from Portsmouth to Nottingham, Derby, Sheffield and Birmingham, although some come from further afield.

The range of problems encountered is broad; it includes ill health of all kinds, but extends to poor relationships with others and with God, all sorts of past hurts and present difficulties, and ministry to those who simply wish to see their relationship with God grow deeper.

Teaching days at The Well encourage others to grow as Christians, to minister themselves, and such teaching often extends by request into churches right across the catchment area.

Far from being an Advice Bureau, the Well is set aside for ministering the healing grace of Jesus Christ, through the Holy Spirit, to all who come.

2

THE STORY SO FAR

It was on March 1st, 1993, that I finally put the world of industry behind me and we opened the doors of The Well Centre of Christian Healing in South Wales. The road by which we had reached this point—establishing a place set aside for, and entirely devoted to, healing prayer—had taken over five years to travel. There had been many potholes and cracks along the way, ready and waiting for the wheels of the vision to get stuck in. Among the deeper ruts were my failing eyesight and all the worries and cares about the future of my family. Much of my struggle to reconcile my growing disability with the goodness of God has been set out in my first book *Healing at The Well*. There I describe my downhill journey into despair until, eventually, I found my way to the foot of the cross of Christ, the only place in the world where suffering and love come together. Notwithstanding the disbelief of so many, this is the only place where anything makes real sense—where Jesus Christ and suffering meet head on.

On my spiritual arrival at Calvary, I went from awareness of the *existence* of God to complete awareness of his *presence*—overnight. In that presence I was being loved and accepted with a strength that I had never before experienced. From that moment of revelation onwards, despite my continuing loss of vision, our tiny prayer group found itself being drawn with increasing interest into the world of healing and wholeness. We battled to keep our little group together through many experiences of prayer 'success' and 'failure'. We found all sorts of interesting places in which to hold our prayer meetings—church halls and schoolrooms—until, eventually, we were given a place of our own. It was almost derelict, but we loved it.

After three years of praying for a safe and dedicated place for suffering people to meet with the healing Son of God, the great day had come at last. The Well Centre opened. I suppose we could have had a band, lots of flags and a press launch, but I could not remember Jesus' ministry beginning like that, so we did not try. If this was to be a ministry of availability, then we would just have to sit, and pray, and wait.

My last few weeks in factory life had been largely absorbed in financial planning for this day—and there was no way that we were going to make it! I pored over the figures, with a strong magnifying glass, until tears of tiredness came to my eyes, but I could not make any reasonable sense of them. Everywhere I looked, the red outweighed the black.

We had promised, and committed, resources which we simply did not have. I have never felt so downright irresponsible in my whole life. Waiting at home was an overbearing mortgage which seemed to have a voracious appetite; gas and electricity bills, and—perhaps even worse—there were two young men to get through university, which would be impossible without parental aid. There were no guarantees here at all. I was committed to The Well, with no gainful employment, and consequently with no understanding of what my income would be.

One thought kept pounding away in my head, drowning out the doubts and fears. Something good was going to happen— tomorrow. How that goodness would show itself, I did not appreciate at the time. I imagined that it was something very healing: some vague understanding—vague, but real enough—that God was going to assure me of something very much better than I had ever had before. But it was not just the financial argument which had to be surrendered. The frustration, anxiety and creeping sense of insecurity—all had to be offered up. At the peak of the emotional battle, God's words were quite clear: "I want you to give up working for me, and start working with me."

Once installed in our own premises, we revelled in the joy and pure fun of founding a prayer centre. The spiritual journey had been long and arduous for me, all the way from the tiny beginnings of faith to the enjoyment and warmth of a relationship with the living God. That journey had brought me, together with a few faithful friends, from the back room of a church to this sacred place of prayer. We seemed to have come so far.

Hard work and prayer would eventually see our hopes fulfilled, as God blessed our restoration efforts. We started with rotten floorboards, peeling paintwork, a broken window, and no telephone. There were no curtains at the windows, and the kitchen should have been put out of bounds on health grounds. The lavatories were old, cracked and rusty. If the building looked like anything at all, in those early days, it certainly did not look like a peaceful place of healing—it was more like an insect wildlife reserve!

All the money we had was given to solicitors, to clear the legalities out of the way. If the building was to be made habitable, then the work would have to be done by us, and by us alone. There were days and days of hard work ahead. We were dirty, and broke!

"Oh Lord," I prayed, while digging out a floorboard which almost disintegrated from dry rot, "we came here to work with you, not to scrub floors and paintwork! What will we do after all this hard work, if no-one comes near the place?"

Much more importantly than all the worry and hard work—the people began to come: at first in very small numbers, but the flow gradually increased; and there seemed no end to God's favour towards them. As people began to respond, I was reminded of the wonderful invitation:

> Whoever is thirsty, let him come; and whoever wishes, let him take
> the free gift of the water of life.
>
> *Revelation 22:17b*

There were many miracles in the early years at The Well, and much to give thanks for. It was not that we saw hundreds of people getting up out of wheelchairs, or being healed of medically incurable diseases; we saw our share of such things, but the real miracles were in the strengthening, rebuilding, refurbishing and mending of broken lives to make whole people again—or as whole as we can be in this fallen world.

Although our eyes had been opened wide by the teaching we had received over the years, it was God's grace which made things happen. Solicitors, doctors and drug addicts, airline pilots and single mothers, clergy and housewives; God does not mind who they are, or where they come from.

The Church's ministry of healing and wholeness is not necessarily about making people get better, but about bringing the peace, and knowledge of self-worth, which comes from reconciling yet more of our self to God. In this way, everyone receives a measure of healing, and the thrill is electrifying.

After some months of scrimping and saving, scrubbing and painting, we at last got the place into reasonable condition. The word had begun to spread that we were there and the flow of incomers was settling down to a regular pattern. Things were looking good. Now we could almost look forward to a developing ministry: more folk, with deeper concerns; more aspects of life and healing to learn about; more excitement watching our living God at work through his Son, Jesus.

In *Healing at The Well* I wrote about the absolute importance of 'offering' to God. There is always something to offer back to him—all the things that give us enjoyment and stability in life as well as the bad things. All is material for sacrifice. I knew the truth of this in my personal life, because at the foot of the cross he had exchanged all my fears, doubts and pains for his great peace. His love is amazingly transforming. Now I was to learn something else. Offering prayer is circular. We offer to God something that we have been given, and he turns it into something else, returning it with love. We accept, and say 'thank you'—and then offer it back again. As this happens, his purposes are advanced in the world.

We had offered The Well Centre up to him for his use everyday. Unbeknown to us at the time, God had a plan to turn it into something that we would never have imagined in our wildest dreams. Ministry life at The Well was going to affect much more than the local community.

After all the upheaval of giving up secular employment and starting a prayer Centre, life had begun to settle again at last—all felt well in the kingdom.

God has been so gracious to us, as he is to any caring, praying group. I feel, sometimes, that his mercy, his willingness to bring order back into our bodies, minds and spirits, pours out of heaven under pressure, longing to burst through into our often untrusting lives.

It is with no small pleasure that we can look back over the history of our ministry to date, and remember the wonders he has done, his miracles, and the judgements he has pronounced.

> Give thanks to the LORD, call on his name;
> make known among the nations what he has done.
> Sing to him, sing praise to him; tell of all his wonderful acts.
> Glory in his holy name;
> let the hearts of those who seek the LORD rejoice.
> Look to the LORD and his strength; seek his face always.
> Remember the wonders he has done, his miracles,
> and the judgements he pronounced,
> O descendants of Abraham his servant,
> O sons of Jacob, his chosen ones.
> He is the LORD our God; his judgements are in all the earth.
> *Psalm 105:1–7*

There was the lady who finally banished any doubts we

may have had as to whether non-believers could receive from God. She worked in the local village and confessed in the street to Jean Hadfield that arthritis in her knees meant that she would have to hand in her notice to her employer the following month—all the hours of standing that went with her job were too painful. We prayed in secret for her, and God touched her where it hurt. She now has no pain or any inflammation, and looks forward to a full life at work.

Then there was the lady who came for ministry and left so full of new life that she literally danced her way towards the front door. Twirling around, she tripped and twisted her ankle, falling out onto the pavement. We hauled her back into The Well and sat her down gently, in front of the big cross, to calm her down from the shock. By this time, her ankle had swollen up like a balloon. Seeing this, one team member simply and quietly told it, in the name of Jesus Christ, to go down and return to its proper state. To my absolute delight, the swelling went back down again—right there and then, in front of the eyes of the team.

Tony, a much treasured member of The Well team, came in one evening with a 'frozen' shoulder. His arm was in a sling to keep it from moving, but he still complained that he was in agony.

"Come on you guys," was his entreaty, "someone pray for me, will you?"

When he got up from the kitchen floor, onto which he had fallen as the healing love of God touched him, he removed his sling, waved his arm around in circles to test the freedom in his shoulder, shouted "Praise the Lord", and left.

Happenings like these may seem minor, but they are never small to those who receive them, and they are always exciting to the beholder.

A gentleman came in one evening to ask for prayer for his back. His spine had recently been operated on and he was in considerable pain and discomfort—the surgeon had told him to anticipate problems for at least three months. He came again a week later to thank us, and to tell us what a wonderful time he had enjoyed with his wife, on a week-long 'bed-and-breakfast' walking tour in the Welsh hills!

And so God's grace flows on, endlessly, from a bottomless well.

There was the joy on a granny's face when she came into the office to report that her young grandson had returned to hospital for a 'hole in the heart' operation and had not needed it after all—one of the 'bigger' ones!

God is so attentive towards seemingly 'lesser' ailments as well. One day, a Roman Catholic friend of mine dropped in to The Well for coffee. We were standing talking, just inside the front door, when it burst open. In limped a local Anglican priest.

"My left leg's killing me!" he blurted out. "It's given me a murderous night—I think it's sciatica. Can you guys pray with me about it?"

Standing in front of our big cross, we set to work. I did the more formal Anglican thing and anointed him with healing oil, while my Roman Catholic friend prayed in tongues. How we laughed about it all, afterwards! Our visitor shook his leg, arched his back to left and right, wriggled around a bit, and announced, "Thanks! Feels great! Praise God!" —and left as quickly as he had arrived. When such things happen, we remember, with thanksgiving, the words of the psalmist, which we do well to make our own at all times:

> God is our refuge and strength,
> an ever-present help in trouble.
> Therefore we will not fear, though the earth give way
> and the mountains fall into the heart of the sea,
> though its waters roar and foam
> and the mountains quake with their surging.
> There is a river whose streams make glad the city of God,
> the holy place where the Most High dwells.
>
> *Psalm 46:1–4*

However, while acts of 'straightforward' physical healing still continue to astonish and delight us all, the ministry expanded, through his grace, into far wider and deeper fields of common, human tragedy. Trauma, abuse of all kinds, drug addiction, sexual problems, haunting memories and relation-ship difficulties, as well as a wide range of depressive and stress-based illnesses have all come to flood our ministry at The Well. We continue to be filled with ever greater awe at God's willingness not just to mend our physical damage but to re-build the lives of his children—often so spoiled because we live in a fallen world. And re-build them is exactly what he does.

To let my mind wander back over these past few years is to plunge into a deep pool of delight at the sheer magnitude of our heavenly Father's goodness. I remember the lady who, as a child, pulled a saucepan of boiling oil onto herself from her mother's stove. Only now, in her late fifties, can she do what she always wanted to—reach out and take the elements in Holy Communion. There in my gallery of joyful memories is the lady who can at last drive past a particular wooded spot off the M52 without breaking out into a cold sweat and falling into a panic attack. There, too, are the ones with eating disorders who now have healthy appetites; and the ones who can now sleep for an eight hour stretch without having a single nightmare about Dad.

Over the years behind us has come an increasing flow of the now grown-up, discarded, remnant children of dysfunc-tional families—from broken and insecure homes that are the breeding ground for a myriad of wholeness shortfalls. It is in dealing with this sort of horrific damage that The Well was proving so useful. It is a safe place. The majority of those who long for God's healing grace would not walk up in re-sponse to an altar call in church, or for platform ministry. What is wrong is too private and too deep—and there is too much risk of an emotional breakdown. Those of us who can take advantage of prayer calls from the front are very much in the minority.

How lovely it is to be able to offer to the Lord a safe place, a listening place, a tender and loving place, where men and women can gently bathe their broken portion in his restoring love, and where Jesus can be glorified again in their lives.

3

SETTING OUT

I recall the time when I was growing up—when life seemed so much calmer and less strenuous than it does now. In those days without television, simple amusements provided a great deal of enjoyment. Naturally, all the summers were hot and lasted for ever, and every day was an adventure—my sister and I were out on bicycles, with picnic hampers slung in front of the handlebars. Winter evenings were filled up by doing jigsaw puzzles and listening to the radio. Now, plodding on with the Lord's work of running a prayer centre, once again all was at peace. My spiritual boat lay easily at anchor in the stream of life. Then, just when my existence was beginning to flow with ease, on a rainy afternoon in the hills of mid-Wales, the Lord gave me another, very different, 'jigsaw puzzle' to sort out.

It was three years into the ministry life of The Well Centre. Jean Hadfield and I were lecturing at the Annual Conference for Anglican Renewal Ministries (Wales), held at the Royal Welsh Agricultural Showground, Builth Wells. By that summer, the invaluable Jean had been a member of the team at The Well for nearly four years. She was there at the conference to read passages from Scripture which I needed when speaking; to put up overheads, and to make sure I ate properly—three functions which had not been included in the training of my guide dog, Yates!

The weather was mixed that summer—misty, moist mornings over the surrounding blue-grey hills; showers in the afternoons, high winds and downpours at night. Despite the anticipated August promise of sunshine and warmth, we found that jeans, sweaters and umbrellas became the dress of the day. We ran between buildings and marquees, cafes and chapels, dragging a confused and miserable guide dog with us. This was definitely not doggy weather.

After one lecture on a drippy afternoon we came across an old friend.

"What we need, Mike," said this respected Anglican clergyman from West Wales, "is a Well Centre in our town. Come to think of it," he went on, "we really need one in every town in the country!"

That must have been the last suggestion we needed to hear at that point. The Well had opened two and a half years earlier and, as the Lord had promised, people had begun to come. We had, by then, broken the back of the refurbishing work. We had been through the struggles of decorating, of finding plumbers and electricians, of scrabbling together odd pieces of furniture and light fittings. The roof had been made waterproof and, as far as we were able, we had ensured that paintwork was sparkling fresh. Life at The Well Centre had just begun to smooth out!

We had started each day with prayer, and The Well had been filled with thanksgiving praise every time someone came to seek God in their situation. Even the time we invested in the painting, the scrubbing and the knocking down of walls had been filled with rejoicing and thanks. We had perspired physically, emotionally and spiritually. We had taken the risk. We had done our bit, albeit nervously, to trust in God the provider. We were beginning to get into the swing of it.

The word began to spread. People who were emotionally broken had begun to come. Those who had trouble in relationships came; those with griefs and sorrows of all kinds came to us, seeking God in their pain. Often we sat around the kitchen table after work and marvelled at the grace that pours down from heaven. Never once did we despair. What might have looked like vague promises in the New Testament gained a sharpness as we began to understand their reality. The truth about Jesus Christ came alive for us again and again, and we had constant reminders that God's original promise to us, which he had given on the day the centre opened, was now coming true. A friend had phoned to say that this extract from Scripture had come to her while she was praying for us:

> And if you spend yourselves on behalf of the hungry and satisfy the needs of the oppressed, then your light will rise in the darkness, and your night will become like the noonday. The LORD will guide you always; he will satisfy your needs in a sun-scorched land and will strengthen your frame. You will be like a well-watered garden, like a spring whose waters never fail. Your people will rebuild the ancient ruins and will raise up the age-old foundations; you will be called Repairer of Broken Walls, Restorer of Streets with Dwellings.
>
> *Isaiah 58:10–12*

But was our friend's comment about more Well Centres a call to do it all over again?

The rest of that day had been a busy one. My lectures at the renewal conference were nearing their conclusion. This was the end of a string of five talks on the healing love of Jesus. Not only did we need to find time to pray about the speeches, but there were people to see and listen to, meals to rush for and wet clothes to be dried out. The timing of our friend's remark could not have been more inconvenient. It stopped me in my tracks.

That night I lay awake listening to the summer rain splattering on the half open window, and to Yates as he snored beside me on the floor of the bedroom. At least my loving and trusting guide dog was at peace with the world!

Memory pictures—of the trials and tribulations of starting a prayer centre with, seemingly, no help and support from anyone except the tiny prayer group—flooded through my mind, leaving pools of inadequacy to splash in. My mood matched the weather outside. Unable to get to sleep, I climbed over the slumbering Yates and leaned my elbows on the damp window sill. Listening to the raindrops spattering the path below my window, I wondered whether I was being called to more tears and sore knees, more heart-wrenching listening to the walking wounded, more anguish at the foot of the cross. Could I cope with another Well? Where would I find the staff for such a venture? Where would the money come from this time? Would the local people use yet another prayer centre in whichever town we were being called to? Was I being called, anyway?

We had been so sure that we should not advertise the ministry at The Well, and we were so positive that we had not created it directly for people but for the God we love. If he could then use it for the healing of bent and broken lives, then that would be marvellous—but it was his place, not ours. Advertising would be left to the Holy Spirit.

I stood at the window, elbows wet from the wind-blown rain, wondering if that policy had actually been a 'cop out' of sorts. Perhaps, it was lack of trust? Perhaps, it was lack of self assurance? It may even have been because marketing is a subject that is as alien to me as sky diving.

Whatever it was, it worked. In the end there had been no hype, no great announcements in the Church press, just the Holy Spirit at work. To be truly obedient to our calling we had had to do everything in love and allow the healing peace of God to be spread abroad by him. We had to be faithful and stay there, too.

Then there were the raised eyebrows. Under whose authority did we operate? Where did we train? Were we trying to convince other Christians that they could somehow be empowered to heal the sick?

Then there had crept in a question of my own. Why is it that the *world* does not object to our working with God in this way? Why is it that some Christians can be so accusing and suspicious when someone else is only trying to serve others in love? That came as a painful thought in the depths of many nights. I learned one valuable lesson in those early days—if a servant is true and faithful to the Most High, people may frequently resent that unflinching devotion, because it is a testimony against their own iniquity.

Would I have to go through all those justification speeches again in some other town? My mind moved on, and I began to think about the enormous risk we had taken. Financially speaking, there is not a bank in the world that would have supported the venture. The Bank of Heaven was supplying all our basic needs, and what a wonderful witness that had turned out to be. The huge expense was being carried almost entirely by thanksgiving gifts from those whose lives God was changing. But if he wanted another prayer centre in another town, and I wanted to repeat the same risk, would that mean taking him for granted?

The questions came in showers.

"I took a big risk for you, Lord," I prayed. "You have honoured that risk. Do you want me to go on taking risks like that?"

I came to the conclusion that the priestly remark which had started all this questioning was probably only an offhand comment and meant nothing. Christians love to encourage each other. Perhaps that was all that was meant by his remarks. Then why were they keeping me up so late?

Yates was, by now, in the depths of some exciting woodland with clear running rivers and deserted badger setts. The paws were twitching and the tail was thumping in the reality of his dreaming. His nose was snorting with the joys of freedom. I followed his example after a long and restless prayer.

"Not another one, Lord!" I whined. "Do I have to go through all that again?" God so often seems to answer my questions by asking some of his own. At the precise moment I turned away from the window towards my bed, a Bible verse came tumbling down from the surrounding hilltops:

See, he is puffed up; his desires are not upright— but the righteous will live by his faith.

Habakkuk 2:4

What does it mean to live by faith? How could I do that? I supposed the only true way would be by looking to God in every situation I would have to face, because he is our shield and our defender.

The battle to create something out of almost nothing had not been ours, but his. God is our Father, and he has good gifts for us; nothing that happens to us is without his consent or his knowledge. We need to trust him and know that we are in his hands, even when we are afraid. I was being reminded that there is no fear in love. I needed to surrender my fears and doubts about the future to him. Was he not greater than my fears? This is the God of the impossible; surely he could handle all my concerns.

Although I could feel my drooping eyelids encouraging me back to bed, my mind seemed to wander off on its own path, as can so often happen in the early hours. I was back with Moses and his people in the desert. What was he going to do with them? They had to be fed, and feeding such a large number of people would need a lot of food. It has been estimated that fifteen hundred tons of food would have been needed daily. And they were forty years in the wilderness! They would have needed water, too. If they had only enough to drink and wash a few dishes, it would have taken millions of gallons each day. They had to get across the Red Sea at night. If they had gone on a narrow path, double file, the line would have been eight hundred miles long and have required thirty-five days and nights for them all to get through. So there would have to have been a space in the Red Sea, three miles wide, so that they could have walked five thousand abreast in order to get over in one night. On top of all this there was another problem. Each time they camped at the end of the day, a camp site covering seven hundred and fifty square miles would have been needed. Did I think that Moses worked all this out before he left Egypt? Moses believed in God. God took care of these things for him.

Why should I think God would have a problem taking care of all *my* needs if I set out on a new journey? I would need to have more faith and trust in him, or continue to walk in fear and be tormented. Eventually, deciding against torment, I climbed back over the dog and pulled the duvet up around my ears. After breakfast the next morning, I sought out the friend who had been the cause of my restless night.

"You weren't serious, were you?" This was a statement looking for confirmation, rather than a question. I had hoped he was just joking.

"Oh," he replied, "quite serious. The need that you see cannot possibly exist just in one town! It must be everywhere." He meant it, after all.

What need were we seeing? One or two local church leaders had advised me not to be too expectant. After all, they said, only one per cent of any congregation ever goes for counselling. Was that true, or were they justifying their own lack of vision—or some deep fear of the unknown? I remembered the unspoken thought that had come to mind at the time. I was not in the counselling business—I had found a living Christ who had far more to offer than that. If Christian healing had something to do with curing illness, then my understanding of Christ was turning out to be much bigger than that, too.

Then I encountered two people, whose experience of the Church challenged me deeply. Within five minutes of meeting my old friend, I was approached, very tentatively, by a lady with a question on her mind that was obviously troubling her greatly.

"May I ask you," she enquired quietly, to avoid being overheard, "do you think I'm demonised?"

"Why do you think you might be?"

"They've told me in church." She began to cry, and I sensed a sinking feeling inside.

"Can you tell me what happened?" I tried to encourage her.

"I went forward for prayer last Sunday at the end of the service. I've had depression for years, you know."

"Did they pray for you?" I asked her.

"The pastor looked at me, and called over all the elders

to listen. Then he told them, not me, that I had a spirit of abuse, and they were to watch as he delivered me."

"How awful!"

She went on, "I don't remember much after that. After everyone had gone home I was still sitting on the floor, huddled up against a radiator in the back room. I was still being shouted at by four or five of them."

"Did anything change in you?"

"Not that I'm aware of. In fact, it felt a lot worse. I wanted to kill myself when I got home. I felt so ashamed. Do I still have a spirit of abuse in me?"

My heart sank. Surely the healing ministry of the Church cannot be like this? Jesus came to us as grace and truth; was this how he was being displayed in our churches? One year—and many such stories—later, made me wonder. If that lady had a spirit of abuse, then who was doing the abusing?

On the final day of the conference there was little to do but enjoy, and relax into, the closing worship service, and wait for my wife, Ginnie, to come in the car and take us home. But there was one more request to come.

"I wonder if you could find the time to pray for me? You see, we don't have healing prayer in my church."

Find the time? The thought flashed across my mind that had I been present in a crowd of thousands on a hillside, listening to Jesus, I would have felt I was the only one there. I wondered if he can only count people one at a time!

A spear shaft of anger rose up from somewhere deep inside, and I had to swallow hard to prevent it shooting out of my mouth. Why cannot all these so-called shepherds offer a little healing prayer to their flocks? How can any church leader suggest he is a pastor and not offer healing prayer? Why are so many of them so blind that they cannot see the sea of pain in their congregations? I swallowed hard again.

Looking back now at that summer week in Mid Wales is to see my clergy friend painting the picture on the front of a jigsaw box: it was a map of the UK, covered in Well Centres. God had then lifted one corner of the lid and allowed me to peek inside. The two people who had come to ask for help on the closing days of the conference might not have been a cross-section of the Christian Church. God shows us these things not to provoke us into anger with the Church, but in order to help us discover the meaning of what we see.

These dear people had shown me two pieces of the jigsaw, mixed up and tossed around inside that box. One piece looked like a ministry that was not particularly holy, if not downright dangerous, and the other piece appeared to show an enormous level of ignorance and leadership unbelief. Was this a pattern? Not yet. One thing seemed quite clear: I was taking the first few faltering steps on another journey. Slowly, bit by bit, God was going to undo and re-construct this 'jigsaw', placing each piece together in my mind until, eventually, I would see the picture again, as it began to grow towards its completion.

4

GOING DEEPER

Despite the not-so-gentle prompting of the Holy Spirit in Mid-Wales that year, warning me that I might still have a long way to go, I sensed with considerable joy that The Well Centre was thriving. People were coming. The ministry was deepening. The ministry team was growing, too. Slowly but surely they grew in number—from the original four of us, to twelve. Every Monday morning was an in-house training day, which meant hours of excited learning in the kitchen at The Well.

We were all thirsty for teaching, and travelled back and forth to conferences and seminars. Eagerly, we sat on the edges of our seats; hungrily, we devoured every word and every experience.

As we watched those who came to The Well for God's help, we began to notice that the problems being presented were growing deeper. We had started by praying with folk with ear infections and broken bones that were not healing quickly enough. Painful and troublesome though these things can be, we began to see, over the early years and slowly at first, what might lie behind some of these difficulties.

As Jesus touched us and others at our points of need, it

became increasingly important to see those who come with the eyes of Christ, rather than simply responding to the initial request. We began to search for the root causes of problems, instead of skimming over the surface of damaged lives with quick healing prayers. We did not want to be dishers-out of 'cheap grace'.

Not long after we opened up the building for ministry, we met a group of three wonderful people—whom I shall call Dorothy, Peter and Jennifer (not their real names).

Dorothy came trundling into the healing service in her wheelchair, sticks across her lap. "I have terrible back pain, I can't stand up straight," she told us. It had been that way for some years. She had undergone various operations, in which her doctors had seen a possibility of helping her, but it was all to no avail. Out of the wheelchair she could take only a few steps before the pain came rushing in again, and she would have to sit down. Had she been anywhere for ministry before? She said that she had, and then added that she was getting nowhere. Lovely Christians had prayed for physical healing, and one minister had actually tried to deliver her of a demonic spirit of backache. God, in her opinion, seemed not to be very bothered about her condition.

We gave her time to talk, and over a hot cup of tea she told us her story. She had been evacuated to Wales as a child during the Second World War. Her mother had brought her down from London on the train, and handed her over to her new guardian at the station. Promising to see her soon, her mother climbed back onto the next London train, and did not return. The family was never re-united. Happily, Dorothy had grown closer and closer to her new Welsh mother who, within a very short period of time, earned the title 'mummy'.

Life goes on. Dorothy grew up, married, and brought two babies of her own into the world. All this time, she was drawn tighter and tighter to her Welsh 'mummy'. Losing one mother at such an early age creates a black vacuum in the child-like soul. Any suitable replacement is readily drawn into that vacuum—and is hung on to for dear life.

All was wonderful until, in her old age, her adopted mother died. The funeral had been the place of pain, the moment her back had given up.

As she bent over the open grave, letting her tears fall down onto the coffin of her rescuer, her 'saviour', she cried out, "I will never leave you!" She could not straighten up again. She was locked in that position. No movement was possible without extreme pain. It felt as though her whole personality had screamed out to stay by her mother's grave. It seemed that her body had simply agreed with her emotions, fixing her to the spot.

Doubts ran through my mind. I could not imagine there being a medical issue here, but who was I to diagnose? Should she seek professional counselling? Would Jesus help her? We talked about it for a while, and then we prayed together. After a long battle with her own emotions, Dorothy forgave her London mother for the desertion, and even forgave her Welsh mother for dying and leaving her. Only then was the blocked grief released. The carpet was soaked with her tears. As her back began to straighten, so her grief began to form. Blocked for all this time by physical back pain, and her need to be strong in the face of suffering, she was now able to release her tears to Jesus. We heard from her again a few months later. Dorothy had got out of bed in the early morning, to go to the bathroom. It was only when she got back into bed that she realised she had walked upright—there and back—had forgotten her sticks, and had experienced no pain. She had joined the worship group in her local church within a few weeks, and loved to spend an entire church service on her feet—worshipping the God who had touched her, and witnessing to his healing love.

We had our 'failures', though. These were devastating. It is so tempting to go over and over the presenting problem, the points of ministry, the feelings of utter failure and the sense of wanting to give up. All we can do, in the end, is go back to the foot of the cross, pray, and learn.

Peter had been going to church all his life—for as long as he could remember, anyway. In his late fifties he developed a rare wasting disease of the muscles, which had taken a great toll, confining him to a wheelchair and destroying his eyesight completely. He spent his days in a care home and was brought to a healing service by a thoughtful nurse.

It was impossible to understand anything he said. The muscles in his jaw and face were so weak. All that came out was a gurgling sound. He could not lift up his head or hold out his hands to receive whatever the Lord had for him. His whole body sagged in the wheelchair, as if it had no bone structure to support it at all. Saliva dribbled from his half open mouth, and soaked down the front of his sweater. All we could do was to anoint him with oil and pray that God might somehow touch him.

By the end of the service, Peter had left his wheelchair behind and was walking quite happily around the church, waving his arms in the air and reading easily from the hymn book. Worship flowed from his lips. He appeared to be restored completely.

By the following morning, his condition had returned and he was back in the wheelchair, finding any physical movement almost impossible. His sight had gone again, and he had to be lifted up onto his pillows.

We felt useless. We felt we had failed him. We learned then that there is only one place to go when 'failure' rears its ugly head. We returned to the foot of the cross, to ask forgiveness for ourselves.

Many would argue that 'you can't win 'em all!' and many more might say to themselves, 'Well, that's his problem, not ours', but Jesus came to save us, not to condemn.

Peter's sad experience brings fresh understanding of the event recorded in Luke 5:17–26.

One day as he was teaching, Pharisees and teachers of the law, who had come from every village of Galilee and from Judea and Jerusalem, were sitting there. And the power of the Lord was present for him to heal the sick.

Some men came carrying a paralytic on a mat and tried to take him into the house to lay him before Jesus.

When they could not find a way to do this because of the crowd, they went up on the roof and lowered him on his mat through the tiles into the middle of the crowd, right in front of Jesus.

When Jesus saw their faith, he said, "Friend, your sins are forgiven."

The Pharisees and the teachers of the law began thinking to themselves, "Who is this fellow who speaks blasphemy? Who can forgive sins but God alone?"

Jesus knew what they were thinking and asked, "Why are you thinking these things in your hearts? Which is easier: to say, 'Your sins are forgiven,' or to say, 'Get up and walk'? But that you may know that the Son of Man has authority on earth to forgive sins...." He said to the paralyzed man, "I tell you, get up, take your mat and go home."

Immediately he stood up in front of them, took what he had been lying on and went home praising God.

Everyone was amazed and gave praise to God. They were filled with awe and said, "We have seen remarkable things today."

Jesus was responding, not to the trust of the client but to the trust of those who brought the paralysed man. They had acted as his ministers. In response to their faith, Jesus forgave sin; he must have known that something lay behind the illness—something which no one else could see. In the sick man's reconciliation to God lay his physical healing.

Jennifer came to The Well Centre seeking prayer and ministry for all-over-body eczema. It had got such a hold on her that she had to wear a layer of tissue paper against her skin, to keep her clothes from touching and inflaming it. When asked how the illness was, she replied,

"The trouble is, it's so angry!"

'Anger' is usually a word used to describe an emotional state, not a physical one. She was asked what was going on in her life around two years before the diagnosis. The question was asked because stressful situations often take about that time to work their way through the emotions and manifest themselves in physical forms. The 'two year theory' was worth remembering!

It transpired that her elderly father had died in very sad circumstances, which involved a large degree of lack of caring on the part of some who were with him when he died. She was still very upset with them.

It would have been so easy to sympathise with her. The lack of care described in her story was quite sickening. However, the trouble is that sympathy does not heal.

"Where was Jesus at that moment?" she asked in anguish.

"Dying on the cross for the perpetrator," was the reply given.

After a long and thought provoking chat about the nature of forgiveness, which went on for most of the afternoon, a time of confession and repentance followed; and there was acceptance of forgiveness for her own sin of unforgiveness. Prayers for healing followed. Within a month, the eczema had died down to a bearable level, and Jennifer had been asked by her pastor to lead a prayer group in her church. She was thrilled.

Shortly after this, one of the ministers at The Well was asked to visit an old lady in hospital who had been rushed there two days earlier with an exploded ulcer. She was very weak—unable to stand unaided—and was being spoon fed by the hospital staff. The doctors had suggested to the family that she was too old and too weak to be operated on; she might not be able to take the strain.

The minister began a conversation with her, feeling, most unscientifically, that her ulcer might have been connected to 'acid', and then to bitterness, and from there back to lack of forgiveness. This was not some prescriptive formula; he simply felt it in his spirit.

She was very weak. In the course of the conversation, the old lady relayed that she had just received the 'welcome' news of her husband's death. She explained that her husband had left her for a younger woman some forty years earlier, and she had long ago lost all contact with him; the news of his death had reached her through her son.

"I'm really pleased!" she added. "I hope he gets all he deserves." The emotion is understandable, but the sin is obvious.

After a lengthy conversation, difficult with someone so ill, the old lady began to ask God to forgive her husband, and to forgive her for feeling so bitter for so many years. As she did so, the strength began to flood back into her body. Two days later, she returned home with her medication in her handbag and her heart at peace, well able to look after herself again.

Towards the end of that year, I had related various such stories, with the permission of those concerned, at a Teaching Day at The Well. Afterwards, I was approached by a man who asked, "So, not everyone gets healed?"

"No," I confessed, "that's part of the mystery of God."

"Then do you have documentary proof that these people were healed?"

"No, just their witness."

"But they could have just got better naturally!" my questioner went on. "So why do you call them miracles?"

"Because they are miracles to them."

"At least you don't claim to make a difference to everybody!" He was triumphant.

A member of the team at The Well Centre loves to relate this story. One day, a man was walking along a deserted beach. There had been a storm the previous day, and the sand was completely covered with stranded starfish. Every now and then the man bent down, picked up a starfish, and threw it back into the sea. A watcher on the rocks shouted to him, "You're wasting your time! There are millions of them! You've no hope! You cannot make any difference!"

The man on the beach ignored the shouts and walked on. Each time he bent and picked up a starfish, he said quietly to it, "Makes a lot of difference to you though, doesn't it?" —before he tossed it back into the ocean.

The words 'healing', 'salvation' and 'saved' can all be linked back to the same root. It has always distressed me that so many 'informed' Christians claim that they are saved, or will be saved, or are being saved, and yet turn so critically towards those people through whom this salvation is being actively demonstrated.

Since my conversion, I am aware that I have been saved through the reality of the cross: Jesus' saving death. I feel as though I am walking into my inheritance of healing, wholeness and salvation by the grace that has its full and final expression in the cross. It is here that divine love bears the burden of my sin—and the world's sin. It is here that God forgives sin, by way of love, through suffering. While this amazing grace is free, I seem to be growing ever more deeply in awareness that it is not cheap. This is costly grace. The mercy-seat which is the throne of God has been a blood-splattered throne since the days of Moses, when it was first revealed. If I, for one, am going to respond to this costly grace of God, I will have to respond with nothing less than my whole being.

If the loving forgiveness of God sets aside from me the penalty and the curse of the Law, then no longer does the latter govern my (or anyone else's) relationship with God. I find this whole idea intensely exciting, but it cannot mean that any one of us, once forgiven, is free to make off like a lawless prodigal into the far country again! The compulsion of the Law has been removed from me, but only because it has been replaced by the compulsion of love—a love so awesome and compelling that I can answer it with nothing less than my entire surrender.

In the process, my confidence is being shifted entirely away from trusting in my own accomplishments towards trusting in the mercy of God. It is there in that mercy—and there alone—that my hope lies for my own fullness of life, and for the wellbeing of those hurt people who surround me.

I realised from the outset of this ministry, with a sad heart, that there were always going to be doubters, those demanding proof, those who are frightened, and the 'pharisees'. Wherever we went on this pilgrimage road to find the heart of God for his people, we would find the world, and much of the Church, stacked up against us.

Why is it so difficult to sit and accept the grace of God for what it is? Why are we always wanting worldly proof? Why can we not simply be as thrilled as those who receive? These were such heart-breaking questions, when all we ever really wanted was to provide an environment of safety and love, where pain could be exchanged for the peace of God in Jesus through the power of his cross. The fact remains that, even within the walls of our churches, 'the unbelieving mind will not be convinced by any proof, and the worshipping heart needs none.'

As I thought about all this, God's answers to these questions came drifting through the mist of this sadness:

"Do not attempt to justify me, I have no need of justification. It is sufficient for you that the Light has come into the world. Arise and shine!"

5

NO PARKING

Coming home after training days and conferences was a joyful time—it always is. Travelling and meeting new people is often fun, and being privileged to share one's thoughts with others is always rewarding. Coming back again into the world of home and family puts the icing on the cake.

After one such occasion I came back to the house to find something Ginnie and I had not expected—not so soon, anyway. The local authority workmen had descended on the road behind the house while we had been away, and painted the gutters with two yellow lines. We had become a 'no parking' zone.

This was indeed welcome. The cul-de-sac that runs along the back of the house is a narrow one, and leads to the homes of a number of elderly people. Double parking by shoppers along each side of the street only serves to block the flow of traffic, hindering any possible access for emergency vehicles. Over the previous year we had signed a number of locally raised petitions to whoever controls these things. We had wanted these lines for a while. Double yellow strips of paint in the gutters would turn this 'village car park' into a thoroughfare again.

Although tiredness from the previous week away from home was creeping over my eyelids, I sat for a while at my prayer desk with the Lord, before going to bed that evening. Going over in my mind the events of the conference we had just attended, I found myself praying again for the two ladies who had sought me out in the crowd, in the closing stages of that thrilling time at Builth Wells, a few months earlier. I prayed, "What can I learn from this, Lord?"

As I slept that night, I dreamed that I saw the bright yellow lines rise up out of the roadside. They crept over the pavement and ran across the local churchyard. Up the wall they went, and over the roof of the church building, falling down the other side, and away out of view.

Was God hanging a 'no parking' sign over his Church? Or was he hanging it over me? Perhaps that was my message? Perhaps God was trying to get me to move? But I thought I was moving! I remembered then the rainy night I had told him, in as many words, that I had done my bit. The Well was coasting, now. Perhaps my satisfaction was a stopping place, and my heavenly Father was nudging me like a traffic warden: no parking! It is a common Christian temptation to look for 'car parks', and then to remain in them. There is often some experience in our lives that brings us to a place where there is a real danger of stopping the flow of God. When we find it, we tend to stay there. That was the trouble with parked cars along our back road. The parking facility made life easier for the car owners, but it blocked the flow. One of the most common traffic signs is that prohibition of parking, or 'settling down' in the busy streets. I was in danger of forgetting that life with Christ is a road, a pilgrimage into the heart of God, a thoroughfare, where we cannot 'park' and be static. We are meant to keep moving with Jesus. Life goes on in the name of the Lord who said, 'I am the Way....'

I woke that morning to a new found realisation that the Christian Church was never meant to be a multi-storey car park, and The Well Centre was not designed for me as a place to catch some spiritual shut-eye! Some of us, myself included, find it so easy to park our spiritual vehicles in all sorts of places.

Some of us park by our failures. After one setback or another, we sometimes say, 'What's the point of all this?' A few months earlier, a lady had sat crying at the kitchen table in The Well Centre. She had offered herself to the Church for training for ordination, and had been rejected.

"Did they give you a reason?" I asked, longing to find some place of hope for her.

"They asked me about my churchmanship—they wanted me to stick a label on myself."

"You know," she went on, "charismatic, evangelical, traditional, anglo-catholic, that sort of thing."

"Did you tell them?"

"I told them that God was all those things and much more. I want to reach out and enclose all of them in my heart. They turned me down for having such a vague view of God."

She could have given up, but she did not. She moved to a different locality and a different church, and kept on trying. Eventually she was accepted. I know her today as a beautiful shepherd, reflecting the light of Christ into the hurting world that surrounds her.

Many others, perhaps most of us, have had setbacks, too. Come to think of it, none of us learned to walk, ride a bicycle, or swim, without having our share of setbacks.

On the other hand, some of us park in a lay-by called 'success'. This might have been where I was seeking to 'stop my car and enjoy the view'.

After a 'successful' church service or spiritual event, we can easily be tempted to park the car and bask in the afterglow of some achievement or other. It is almost as if we say to ourselves, 'That was superb! Perhaps now we can coast for a while.' The difficulty, which we often fail to see, is that successful coasting is always downhill!

The first couple of years of my teenage life were spent in the estuary village of Noss Mayo in Devon, which I recall as one of the country's loveliest and most unspoiled beauty spots. My mother had bought a rowing boat for the princely sum of twelve pounds, and it rapidly became a waterborne 'second home' for my sister and myself. We had carefully crafted together our own boat anchor from a few heavy bars of rusty old iron and a length of nylon rope. On our first outing to the centre of the Pool (the name given by the locals to the large bulge in the estuary where two rivers meet and the big yachts were moored) we dropped the anchor and sat for a while, admiring the scene. Some time later, when we decided to try a different viewing spot, we pulled on the rope to draw up the anchor. Instantly, we became aware of a serious problem. The anchor we had made was far too heavy, and had sunk into the soft and muddy bottom of the Pool. I remember that, no matter how hard we pulled, we were unable to yank it free. Sometimes, our relationship to our church family is much like this situation. We are encouraged by the Bible to anchor ourselves in the security of having fellowship with other believers. While this, I am sure, is a good and healthy Christian practice, the Well Centre team would have to be equally careful not to become so secure that we would become immobilized—as my sister and I had been in our little boat.

There is a time for 'fellowship' with other believers and a time to 'go ye into all the world'. We should be careful never to allow ourselves to be immobilized by our spiritual security. God was beginning to show me that my anchor was getting stuck in the mud.

The old saying, 'practise what you preach' came to the fore. Quite a number of folk were coming to The Well with griefs and losses of all kinds. Lost spouses, lost careers and lost hopes; all who came longed for restoration. Much of the hope in our hearts would be that they would stand up again with Jesus—and keep moving.

I regularly use one picture to encourage those who are hurt by the pitfalls along the road; it was one I had heard in a sermon, and had stuck like a tiny piece of meat between the teeth. Imagine that you are standing with Jesus. In front of you is a high wall that you cannot see over. As you approach the wall, he helps you climb up and over the wall—and comes with you. That picture reminds us of the close presence of Jesus, even before we are consciously aware of him. In front of us now is a huge field, bathed in the dusky twilight of nightfall. We cannot see the far side, nor anything which is more than a pace in front of us. We walk on, because we have no option. There is certainly no going back. In the field we find discarded and rusty old farm implements, nasty things left by cows, and patches of brambles, full of stinging nettles. We cannot see, and we fall against them and into them, and are driven to our cut and bruised knees. This is life.

We have two options. We can 'lie down and die' in a muddy pool of self-pity, or we can notice that Jesus is still standing there, pierced hands outstretched, longing to lift us to our feet and take us on.

Eventually, after a long time, we reach a high wall at the other end of the field. We have absolutely no idea what lies beyond it, and yet there is Jesus, offering again to help us go forward, and over it. Up and over we go into a new and wonderful kind of daylight—all aches and bruises gone. This is death and resurrection.

We noticed that a few of the people who came to The Well seemed not to want to move from their griefs and sorrows. It was proving well-nigh impossible to help those who wanted a little sticking plaster, a cup of tea and some sympathy, yet had no real desire to get up and move on. I do not mean to belittle the awful blackness and aching hunger of grief, but we do need sometimes to be reminded that Christ is here, too. After Jesus of Nazareth died and was raised from the dead, a messenger said to the grieving women in the garden:

"But go, tell his disciples and Peter, 'He is going ahead of you into Galilee. There you will see him, just as he told you.'"

Mark 16:7

Some sufferers have parked in a place of mourning, and need help to move on from that place.

There is no need to 'park' ourselves beside the silent

dust, and weep for ever. In church, or family, or at work, we look from a short distance at what might have been, and see what appear to be empty shells of history. Should we crawl back into them, or walk gently away? We can 'have the mind of Christ' about life. Part of the significance of this is that even when going through the 'valley of the shadow of death' we are not to park there; and we can know that he is with us, accompanying us all the way.

Sometimes, I have been guilty of parking in spiritually significant moments, too. After a 'good' church meeting, we long to return for another. After an exciting conference we look forward to next year's. We park our cars alongside spiritual moments.

I was beginning to find much of the activity in the renewal movement in the Church to be like this. Some of us have to admit that fine worship, singing, good teaching, and a dose of ministry, elevate the soul back up to where we were the last time we met together for such a purpose, but that we are almost 'coasting' in the in-between times. We need to return to his glorious presence every day. These corporate Christian activities are good, obedient responses to the grace of God, in which he often moves powerfully amongst his people. But we are sometimes guilty of thinking that his healing grace puts us 'back where we were'. Rather, he wants to use the special moments to draw us into a closer daily walk with himself.

Consider the account of Jesus' transfiguration, recorded in Mark 9:2–9. Jesus had taken his friends, John, James, and Peter, to a mountain. The Greek term for transfiguration is 'metamorphosis'. This is a change of form, appearance or nature. A tadpole undergoes metamorphosis in becoming a frog. A caterpillar travels through a metamorphosis to become a butterfly. Through being born again of the Spirit of God, we begin to 'glow'.

On the mountain, with his friends, the watchers saw Jesus in a new light—literally, as Jesus' divine glory shone out from his human flesh and bone, and his clothing became glistening, dazzling white.

Moses and Elijah, men who had lived centuries earlier, appeared with Jesus. By allowing the disciples to see them, God taught them a wonderful truth about the promise of eternal life, transcending this life. Peter, watching, then spoke:

> Rabbi, it is good for us to be here. Let us put up three shelters— one for you, one for Moses and one for Elijah.
>
> *Mark 9:5*

Peter wanted to park by that spiritual experience and stay there. In effect, however, Jesus gave him the same message that I was receiving through those thoughts about double yellow lines: no parking!

Surely, I wondered, our special, spiritual moments are not to be the goal of the religious life; rather, they are the gateways to even fuller, richer and longer lasting moments of closeness to God.

Where is the exit from whichever 'car park' we find ourselves drifting into? We search for new and exciting church projects, the raising up of ministries, the involvement in community affairs, the public display of signs and wonders. We may take up good causes and become campaigners for what is 'right'. Yet even in the midst of such activities, good in themselves, we may miss the way of God.

So which way did he want this one to go? Did he want more Well Centres —or not? I thought of 'putting out a fleece', but that is not commended in Scripture as part of normal Christian decision-making, so I decided against doing so. We want so much to know what God's will is in a given situation that we catch ourselves thinking, 'If I do this, and the pastor does that, then I shall know that God wants me to go down this particular road.' But Gideon knew full well what he had to do: he had already been told.

A week later, I phoned the friend we met at Builth Wells, the one who had started all this searching, and asked, "Peter, what was behind your comments about wanting a Well in your town?"

"Oh," he was not hesitating, "my heart is just longing

to see the church put into the community, not the other way around. So many churches are trying to become places of community, inviting others in. In our next-door parish they've made their church building smaller and put in a community room, some lavatories and a kitchen. They're going through all the business of getting grants for the work and they're just hoping it will be used."

"Sounds very practical to me!" I replied.

"Yes," he went on, "but for me it's the wrong way round. I don't want our church to be thinking of ways to 'bring people in' —other than our evangelism, of course. I want to somehow pick up church and take it to the community in some way which is important to them."

"But Peter," I argued, "the country is littered with congregations doing good works in the community!"

"I don't know if I can find the words to explain myself," he apologized. "You see, I want us to take Jesus to them, not just do good things which are mostly not recognized as being Jesus."

I tried to understand him. I think he was saying that 'good works' which do not attract people to Jesus may be good servanthood, but are not seen as the light of Christ. The light is in the world, but the world will simply go on not seeing it. Church, to much of the world, will go on being a charitable fixture of some kind.

"I'm not sure," I said, trying to find excuses, "that a Well Centre would be your answer. We tend to minister to Christians and those on the margins of faith. We don't see many non-Christians."

"Fine!" came the reply. "Who should the centre shine the light on first, but those on the edge?"

6

ARISE AND SHINE

Remembering that phone call with my friend Peter, the word 'shine' stands out. What was its significance? The Church is sent into the world as a means for worship and proclamation. For any church, in an inward-looking frame of mind, to imagine that it is the final goal of God's purposes would be the great denial of her mission. She is meant to reveal and proclaim the 'light of the world'. Do we bring light to those around us? Still slightly confused by all this, I left it with the Lord and got on with the daily business of running a healing Centre.

Three days after my garbled conversation with Peter, the phone rang in the middle of supper. It was my bishop. He was going to the Lambeth Conference, and wanted a collage of our work, mounted on a presentation board, to display some of the mission work that was going on in the diocese.

"But, bishop," I wanted to get this right, "The Well Centre is not a piece of mission."

"Yes it is!" came his assured reply. "Anyone who takes God out of the church building is a missionary."

I had a bit more of the answer—another piece of the jigsaw. I still had no idea how it would all fit together, but it sounded as though we were on the right lines. This scripture came to mind:

> I gain understanding from your precepts;
> therefore I hate every wrong path.
> Your word is a lamp to my feet and a light for my path.
>
> *Psalm 119:104 –105*

I pictured a man walking up a lane in the dark depths of night, and thought: if he carried a lantern it would only show him one pace in front, one to the rear and one to either side. So I resolved to keep my spiritual eyes open and my feet moving, and see where God was leading me.

The questions were still there. Arise, where? Go and do what, exactly? I thought, 'I was going the right way with you, Lord.' And shine? That word 'shine' really felt as if it might be another piece of the jigsaw puzzle. I slipped it 'into the box' with the others and paid little heed to it. Life was too busy.

We had to face up to a difficult decision. The Well Centre was thriving, but it was a stand-alone operation. It was not, formally, an outreach project of the Church; it was not an activity going on in the local church hall. It was not under the authority that it should have been. In one sense, I felt secure in the knowledge that Christ is the head of the Body, and we were a part of it. In another sense, I felt a little uneasy because we were unable to demonstrate to other Christians that we were not 'lone rangers', shooting off at a tangent. Then, in a flash, came what seemed like the answer: we would find a clergyman to head up the team. The Trustees could not afford to offer a salary, but then we had taken financial risks before. We could not have found him a house either, but the Lord would, we hoped, provide. With the approval of the Trustees behind me, I began to look around.

I made lists of retired pastors, but they had all retired! I made lists of the ones with no money, but they were too poor to come. We advertised in the church press, but to no avail. What, I wondered, was God doing? I could only conclude that he was making me wait for the right person to become available. Then, one late summer evening, walking home from The Well, I knocked again on the gates of heaven:

"Lord, show me the man! Help me to see the one you've chosen for us!"

I knew in the deep reaches of my being that a provision had been made; a clergyman would be provided. It was probably just my lack of vision that prevented me from coming across God's choice. What had I missed? Where else was there to look?

Soon after this, it was time for my regular trip to see the bishop. I had fallen into the more than pleasant habit of turning up on his doorstep every six months or so, to keep him informed and, hopefully, to drink a cup of his coffee. A few days later found me sitting in his rocking chair. My guide dog, Yates, lay at my feet, keeping a watchful eye on the coffee table because of the plate of biscuits that, in his view, dominated it!

We talked a while. The bishop spoke of Jesus, with a love that was obvious —a real tonic. He encouraged me, as he always does, assuring me that I was, indeed, going the right way. I waited for the conversation to open up an opportunity for me. I wanted to enlist his help in the search for the elusive 'reverend leader'.

Towards the end of our time together, I was on the point of broaching the subject when he asked, "Would you like me to ordain you?"

My mind went into a spin. Where did that come from? I remember feeling so grateful that his rocking chair has arms, because without them I would have fallen off!

"You can't just do that!" I stumbled.

"There may be a way."

"But, I'm too old!"

"I know how old you are."

"I can't see well enough to study, I'm blind!"

"True."

"I don't want to leave my work and go to theological college for three years." I fought on.

"I don't want you to." I was beginning to lose the

battle. All my arguments were being shot down as fast as I could raise them.

In a final attempt to conclude the conversation, I said, "But I don't want to go through that selection process. I did it years ago and got rejected. It was awful!"

He had his answer to that one, too. "I've just selected you." He finished our talk by adding, "Ordination won't open many doors for you, but it will certainly oil the hinges!"

I bumbled out into the sunshine, leaving behind some vague remark about needing to pray about it. Perhaps we could meet again soon and discuss it further. It had not dawned on any of us that God's answer lay, as it so often does, right under our noses. This would take some thinking about.

I went home to tell Ginnie what the bishop had said. She sat me down on the garden seat outside the back door with another mug of coffee, and then left me to start thinking it all through. Now was the time to reflect seriously upon what ordination might mean.

These verses came straight into my mind:

> ...now that you have tasted that the Lord is good. As you come to him, the living Stone—rejected by men but chosen by God and precious to him—you also, like living stones, are being built into a spiritual house to be a holy priesthood, offering spiritual sacrifices acceptable to God through Jesus Christ.
>
> *1 Peter 2:3–5*

So, I pondered, we are not only to be 'holy people' but a 'holy priesthood'. In this expression, we move from what we *are* to what we *do*. Are our clergy intended to be merely decorative? I could not stand being that! Reading that scripture again, it seemed to me the idea of a 'royal priesthood' was not addressed just to the leaders of the congregations, but to the congregations themselves. Should not Christian priesthood be a function of the faith community as a whole? I could not find any instance in the New Testament where an individual Christian is described as a 'priest'. Jesus Christ himself is the great High Priest; and nowhere is the term 'priesthood' applied to a special group within the Church.

The whole community of saints seems to be 'priestly' in character, by virtue of the relationship of Jesus to his body, his people. This notion of priesthood has always been basic to my understanding of the Church, and I take it to be true to the teaching of the New Testament.

This doctrine is sometimes referred to as 'the priesthood of all believers', but perhaps that term fails to encompass the New Testament concept adequately. Some people seem to associate the idea with their right to vote at church meetings. In some denominations, it would appear that the idea was lost altogether in the setting up of a special professional group in the Church. Did my bishop want me to join some special elite group, to whose hands alone was entrusted the power of God? Surely not. For the New Testament speaks of Christians—not just leaders; not only the ordained ministers, but all those for whom Jesus, the Lamb of God, was slain—in these terms:

> You have made them to be a kingdom and priests to serve our God, and they will reign on the earth.
>
> *Revelation 5:10*

It seemed to me that the understanding of 'priesthood' clearly conveyed by the New Testament is *not* that every person can be his or her own 'priest', nor is it even that each Christian must be a 'priest' to his or her fellow Christians, though the requirement for mutual service and self-giving love in the body of Christ has a bearing on the matter. I began to understand more clearly that each believer somehow shares in the priesthood which is the characteristic of the Church as a whole. Looking at this from a different point of view altogether, I remembered that bishops or 'overseers' were a vital element of the structure of the early church, and the office of elder, presbyter or church leader evolved into the 'clergy' of later periods.

As all these reflections, prompted by the bishop's words, went on in my mind, another jigsaw piece was struggling to drop into my outstretched hands. It occurred to me that, in this matter of ordination, individualism may be foreign to the spirit of the Bible. Certainly, we do not need a human priest to act as an *intermediary* between us and Christ for our salvation, nor for our continuing growth in the Christian faith and life. Christ is our mediator, and we have access to his throne of grace and mercy. When I came to Christ as an individual, I felt incorporated into his body—not as an isolated unit, but as one of a group of 'living stones'. The stress ought to be on our interdependence, not our independence. The Well had to become an integral part of the Body, part of this royal priesthood. We wanted to offer spiritual sacrifices acceptable to God through Jesus Christ. But, I wondered, what does this holy Christian priesthood—all of us together in the Church, that is—actually *do*? What are these sacrifices that Peter tells us that we should be offering through Jesus Christ? In Revelation 8:3, I discovered, the saints—the 'holy ones'— are offering up their prayers:

> Another angel, who had a golden censer, came and stood at the altar. He was given much incense to offer, with the prayers of all the saints, on the golden altar before the throne.

The sacrificial prayers of Christians are heard in heaven and make a difference! With such sacrifices of praise, God is well pleased. In ancient Israel, the sacrificial system, given by God under the old covenant, prefigured the new covenant, under which Jesus himself was the one, full, perfect and sufficient sacrifice for sin. Offering our sacrifice of praise includes giving him all that we are and everything we do, in love and obedience.

These somewhat convoluted thought patterns were to serve me later in teaching about the corporate holiness of the Church; understanding the reality of it was another important piece of the jigsaw. Above all, it became clear to me that it is the *whole* body that Christ is calling to shine, not just its leaders.

So, was I being called to be a clergyman? Not if it just meant being licensed to bury the dead and take church services! I wanted to be in my jeans, on my knees before the throne of grace, up to my eyeballs with ministering to people who were in pain. That was where I felt at home. That was my calling.

By now I had discovered that, although the gifts of the Holy Spirit are wonderful, and are such a vibrant witness to the presence of the living God, the greatest gift I could ever have would be that of bringing others into the divine presence. After that, what happens is between God and the sufferer. If that is priesthood I could be prepared to receive it!

By the time my six-monthly trip to the bishop's house came around again, I had studied, mentally fought over, argued about, and tried to rationally discuss, many aspects of ordination in the Anglican Church. Above all, it would give the team at The Well the one thing we had wanted and felt was appropriate: it would place us under proper authority. As part of my preparation for that day, I contacted a number of clergymen around the country, asking them the same question: "What does Ordination mean to you?"

The answers were various, and this variety did not really help at all. On the one hand I was told, "Just go out and have a few beers the night before. Enjoy it!"

From the other end of the spectrum came a statement which startled me: "Ordination will make you holy!" Did this mean something would change? Hurriedly, I asked the gentleman, "How do you define holiness?"

"A holy person is someone who is set aside for God." That could mean anything. Putting down the phone, I sighed, collapsing back into my chair.

I could say, then, that ordination simply makes me a full-time church official. Was that all it would be? There had to be more. I did not know it then, but that conversation was to switch on a new light, an enormous desire to seek the true meaning of the word 'holy' and to search for it for myself. In the end, the search for holiness was to become everything for me; without holiness, nobody would see the Lord. We had searched for an authorised leader, and God was going to give us one. Eventually, the long awaited day arrived. The day chosen for my ordination was the same date as that set for the first ordinations of women in Wales to the priesthood, so I had opted out and persuaded the bishop to delay a week. That particular day was their day, their special time, and I felt that it should be left to them.

A week later, with all the arrangements made, the great day was upon us. My tummy wobbled and my knees shook. Notwithstanding all my thoughts about the corporate character of ministerial ordination, something in me wanted a private affair, just family and friends, but it was not to be.

I stumbled out of the vestry at the back of a long procession of choristers, hanging on to the elbow of the local parish priest (in the absence of my guide dog) and felt quite overcome by what I found. There were hundreds of people present! By the time the procession reached its destination, the worship had nearly lifted off the roof. The joy that rolled around that church was immeasurable. I cried all the way through.

The service was over in a flash, or so it seemed at the time, and soon afterwards we were back at The Well Centre, to entertain those who had come.

Funnily enough, my most abiding memory of that occasion is of something which occurred afterwards. One of our sons had driven home quickly, to fetch my guide dog, Yates. Rushing into The Well, Yates caught sight of me across the room. Suddenly, this huge Labrador crashed into my chest, and wrapped his front legs around my neck, his tail going round like a helicopter propeller blade. He said it all!

7

EXPLOSION

Before another six months had gone by, there were two noticeable changes at The Well. For some unknown reason, the word had spread remarkably rapidly. More and more people made the trip to South Wales.

It was not just that we were becoming busier, receiving travellers from further afield, the atmosphere in The Well was changing, too. It was not only me and the team that felt it—remarks about the atmosphere being somehow 'different' became commonplace, even amongst those visitors who did not profess Christianity. This change was to play on my mind for months, teasing me into an eventual recognition of its spiritual content.

For the time being, however, we had work to do. Until then, our catchment area had covered only the south-eastern corner of the principality. From across that small quadrant came every type of person, all treated the same, all accepted and loved and all very different from each other. But, in the space of only a few weeks, people started arriving from the north of Wales, the Midlands and the south east of England. Even a few missionaries returning home on leave were making a beeline for The Well, to collapse in Jesus' lovely

59

presence. Were all these people 'weirdos'? No—they were God's children, in need of his love and help. They came with illness, of course. They came with emotional and relationship problems, some of which might seem to be of little account and some that seemed huge. To each person, their difficulties were insurmountable without the help of our loving Father in heaven. One way or another, God touches all.

This surge of interest presented me with a problem: there were simply not enough staff at The Well to cope with it. Those sitting on the edge of the team and looking on with interest were called in, put into training and used as back-up in ministry sessions. When that was not going to be enough, I sat and panicked before the Lord. I hated the idea of having to tell people to wait for appointments—Jesus would never have done that! However, God was good to us and supplied, just in time, all our needs. I remembered the earlier comment I had heard, that only one percent of our congregations went for counselling. Talking with those who came to The Well, we began to see why. There seemed from their comments to be three main reasons for that assumption. Firstly, we found a conviction in the Church that counselling, whether it is called Christian or not, is a secular skill and, not to put too fine a point on it, a last resort before the outpatient department of the local mental hospital. Secondly, the expectation of the local churches, and presumably, therefore, others as well, was that the healing ministry is for physical illness and then only if the medical profession is not succeeding. Prayer for healing was regarded by many as a 'hit and miss' affair. This is not at all surprising. Much of what passes for healing ministry appears shallow, lacking in grace, and fails to express the love of the Lord. A remarkably high number of folk were coming to tell us how angry they were at being delivered of yet more demons, which were probably not their problem in the first place. Thirdly, and most sadly, those needing God's help were not, by and large, confiding in their pastors, elders and vicars. Reasons given for that were manifold, but centred around lack of confidence in them, and lack of trust in confidentiality.

In truth, we were finding that only a small percentage of the needs of congregations are purely physical problems. I could not, at first, believe the vast scope of God's grace, but the width and depth of his help was reaching into so many dark corners, kept away from the glare of the observation of others; kept in the home and the heart, not to be shared.

Many—perhaps most—of those who work in the field of healing prayer, get frustrated by the lack of witness about physical healing. Even when things which we may want to term 'miracles' do occur, there seems to be a tendency in some areas of the medical profession to dismiss the idea. There is also the concern that not everyone could get healed through our prayers or the laying on of hands because then the whole world might beat a path to our doorstep, and then who gets the glory? Would it be us, or the local ministry team; the local church, or Jesus? I suspect it would not be Jesus, but then thousands in need flocked to him in New Testament times— not because they were all aware that he was the Son of God, but because they knew he could heal folk. They had an expectancy about his healing power, whilst not necessarily acknowledging who he was.

I wonder, sometimes, just how high a level of expectancy of God is abroad in the Church generally, today. When it comes to the physical side of healing, we probably keep much of our expectancy for our wonderful doctors and nurses. Quite properly, we place a great deal of trust in them when we need their skills. But it is our lack of expectancy about *what God can do* that is at least part of the reason for the 'shortage' of miracles. But can we really speak of a shortage? There is actually a known, visible outpouring of God's love into our bodies in healing ways, through the Church; a miraculous abundance of grace is experienced. More people than we can count do receive a whole or partial healing through prayer. It is only our low expectancy level that means we do not always receive all that God has in store for his children.

Expectancy may be low in much of the Church (in the Western, industrialized world at any rate) but the need for divine healing of all kinds grows continually. We see the loss of so many values, breakdown in the structures of family life, more stress and strain in everyday living, the collapse of many marriages, and an ever-increasing thirst for the occult. All this takes a huge toll on physical, emotional and spiritual life.

'Don't worry about the children. They'll probably adjust to the divorce more quickly than the parents.' Some twenty-five years ago, this used to be the popular idea about the effects of divorce on children. Today, there is a growing body of research, clinical observation and ministry experience, which amply demonstrates that, in many cases, parental divorce has a devastating long-term effect on children as they go on through life into adulthood. The practical experience of both counsellors and ministers is showing that, at any age, stretching or breaking a parental attachment can easily set a child up for the possibility of serious emotional and behavioural problems later in life. We so often see this in people who have had one or both of their parental attachments stretched or broken by adoption, divorce, abuse or neglect when they were young.

Nowadays, the little team at The Well is learning that anything which stretches or breaks the attachment to a parent before adulthood has the potential to project children back to the beginning and cause them, when they grow up, to respond to other people around them with mistrust instead of trust. This often affects children and adolescents, leading to shame and doubt, guilt, inferiority, and some identity confusion. This may, in turn, easily lead to the serious behavioural and emotional problems commonly identified as 'attachment disorder'. Because divorce stretches or breaks the attachment to at least one parent, it has the potential to cause dysfunctional behaviour and thinking in the child. This sort of behaviour and these thought patterns are frequently carried on into adulthood.

None of us should use such understanding of our early years to excuse our behaviour or justify our adult inability to form deep and long-lasting relationships. What we began to find, though, was that such insights help the minister to pinpoint sources of anger and mistrust. When the point of pain can be recognised, then the minister may encourage real confession, the giving and receiving of forgiveness, and the healing that flows from it.

Linda was pregnant and in her thirties, ready to divorce David, who had been her husband for over nine years. Apparently attractive and obviously intelligent, she had little or no confidence in either of those gifts. She came into The Well Centre like a whirlwind, glaring suspiciously out from under lowered eyelids. Living in the terribly distressing fear of being abandoned by her husband, she said, "I'm not wondering if David will leave me, I just want to plan for it and be certain I'm ready when he does." Even the smallest disagreement at home put her immediately on the attack, and she found herself demanding instant solutions to any problem that arose. Whenever David needed a little time to think about a problem and work out the best solution for them, Linda would interpret his hesitation as not caring enough about her or their relationship. She was spontaneous and explosive, to the point of being completely irresponsible, and she had simply no idea that her actions were themselves the cause of the problem. David was giving off strong signals that enough was enough.

We knew we had to help Linda to see herself as a person of worth and value, who did not need to protect herself in this way from her perceived abandonment by David, or anyone else. It was only through prayer and the graceful ministry of the Holy Spirit that Linda began to see the real source of her anger, which had been so frequently and unfairly directed at her husband.

Linda's anger was pointing, deep down somewhere inside, to the long-ago divorce of her parents and what she understood as the abandonment of her by her father in the process. "I'm all alone in the world," she said. "Because I'm not certain who will always be here to take care of me, I've just had to learn to take care of myself." When we learn to walk through life with Jesus, this no longer has to be true for any of us. There is no therapy—medical, fringe medicine, new age, occult, nor any form of counselling—that can come near the fullness of healing afforded through the cross by the living Christ. There is only Jesus, and his 'success rate' in permanently mending this type of damage is extraordinary.

We need to open up the Church's ministry to the possibility of the Lord being active and working on the roots of such things in family life. We also need to recognise that at the heart of our ministry is not only the desire to see folk get better, but also to see the kingdom grow by reconciling our deep bits inside to God—for *this* is where we find the real power of the Lord, the message of the cross, today. In this area, there is almost no witness going on at all, for reasons which may be obvious to the reader, as they affect the most private parts of people's lives. What there is in this 'kingdom work' is the wonderful thrill of seeing Jesus extend his kingdom in individual lives, every day of the week. The 'recipients' of ministry become witnesses in the Body of Christ, just because they become sharper reflections of the light of Christ to each other and to the world. They grow a little more holy.

We witness, too, by persevering in faithful prayer despite the frustrations! Quietly and gently, the good Lord is working miracles all day long in people's kitchens and living rooms, in Christian centres of all sorts—and much of it is outside the local church, in the mission street, where life really hurts; in places where people can talk, and where hurt people who really need him find they can express their need.

Those who take their ministry out of the local church into the community rarely have time to stop for breath. If they do, they only gasp it out again in wonder!

Dr. George Carey, Archbishop of Canterbury, recently said, "A healing church is not one where everybody gets better. It's a church whose congregation is desperately concerned with the well-being of those around it."

In all this, The Well Centre had become a safe place, somewhere to let pain rise up to the surface, where the Lord could deal with it. Into that place of safety came the married couples fighting to save their marriages. We saw beautiful saints with no sense of self worth, church leaders who had lost their direction and had no one to share their pain with. The troubling memories that destroyed any attempt at relationship building were there. Those suffering from all kinds of sexual brokenness, depression and a myriad of what are probably stress-related concerns came, too.

Right from the beginning we had abandoned any technique that was not saturated with the love of Jesus, his gentle acceptance and longing for his sheep that may have fallen off the path. And we discovered early on that, real as demonic oppression can be, there were not demons lurking everywhere!

It was, and is, an enormous privilege to be there, and available for people, in this way. But we had to help them— really help them. So-called 'Christian sympathy' is not healing. Listening and agreeing that people should be hurting after all that has happened to them is not healing. This is 'cotton wool ministry' and serves no one. The Good News of Jesus Christ is poised behind every door to every room in every life.

The team at The Well had studied hard. Courses in this kind of ministry had, by now, become commonplace. We began to grow in the use of the charismatic gifts of the Holy Spirit, and saw many results that simply flabbergasted us. But it never felt like enough; there had to be more.

When we found the key, the floodgates opened. It was when we discovered the road we were to tread that the catchment area exploded. Suddenly, God's troubled children were coming to The Well from all over Wales, the West Country and as far afield as London, Manchester and Birmingham. We lost all pretence of being an offshoot of the local parish church. We were no longer local but national. We dispensed with the idea of just having a small chapel, and set out some comfortable chairs and one or two sofas in the big conference room, around the cross there. What had been our tiny chapel was converted into an office, to handle this new level of throughput.

What was this key? What was it that turned the whole thing upside down? Was it my ordination? Had we somehow suddenly gained credibility through that? Was it our training that was bearing fruit at last? We were not advertising; we were not 'evangelising' the healing gospel of Christ. We did not have long strings of speaking engagements or literature mail shots. These dear ones were finding their way to The Well without any prompting from us at all. It took us a while to find the answers. We discovered that the key to effective ministry is twofold. We needed to understand that ministry is **finding and following what Jesus is already doing**, and we started to realise that the greatest gift of all was not the prophetic words, nor the power of deliverance—it is the God-given ability **to bring others into his presence**.

I would like to write that it was as simple as that, but both these insights had to be sought; both are roads that have to be travelled.

We should be continually reminding ourselves that every Christian is primarily a *disciple* of our Lord Jesus Christ. We all need to grow from being converts to being disciples. This discipleship has to be maintained throughout our lives through prayer, worship and the study of Scripture—the driving force being the need to deepen our own relationship with God. Without this prayer, study and worship, our discipleship, and many of our church projects, will fade away. We Christians tend to become pilot lights, when we are called to be a furnace! The result of our discipleship should be that we continue our own walk through life, but in a particular and noticeable fashion—the way of God.

Most Western Christians are involved in churches that are not growing numerically. Many of our leaders feel they are failures. But they may well be more 'successful' in God's eyes than others whose churches are blossoming, but whose growth may be simply catering to the leadership egos. We must be so careful of that impostor 'success'. We may succeed—but it seems to me that God's will is that we shall not need to be successful to be happy.

We learnt that if we were becoming over elated by our 'successes' in an expanding ministry, or downcast by any apparent 'failures', then we still had plenty of maturing to do! The way of God often appears to be the way of weakness. A large part of the great news of the gospel is that God, in the shape of a human being, became vulnerable, and in that vulnerability bore such healing fruit among his people as the Holy Spirit moved, revealing the Father's heart of compassion. There is power at work, but a power that looks very different from worldly 'power'.

The second key that came to us in those days was a flickering light as we began to see the significance of **servanthood**. God alone was exalting the ministry at The Well, precisely because we had not looked for it.

> Jesus called them together and said, "You know that the rulers of the Gentiles lord it over them, and their high officials exercise authority over them.
> Not so with you. Instead, whoever wants to become great among you must be your servant, and whoever wants to be first must be your slave—just as the Son of Man did not come to be served, but to serve, and to give his life as a ransom for many."
>
> *Matthew 20:25*

In today's world, to become great means to be the best, to be the first, to become a leader. To be great means that we are pushing towards the top; other people serve us, and we may think we have every right to be proud, and even arrogant. Once we become 'the greatest' we may expect people to meet our every need, to flock towards us, and to make way for us.

Christian leaders and concerned friends were asking, "How's The Well? Do many come these days?" No doubt such enquiries are meant kindly, but they signified that people wanted to evaluate our success.

Our only answer was this: "They come one at a time."

It simply does not work any other way. In God's kingdom, to achieve greatness we become servants. We lay to one side our own desires and plans, and focus on the interests of others. This means being humble, and obedient to the will of God. Philippians 2:3–9 makes this clear:

> Do nothing out of selfish ambition or vain conceit, but in humility consider others better than yourselves. Each of you should look

not only to your own interests, but also to the interests of others.

Your attitude should be the same as that of Christ Jesus:

Who, being in very nature God, did not consider equality with God something to be grasped, but made himself nothing, taking the very nature of a servant, being made in human likeness.

And being found in appearance as a man, he humbled himself and became obedient to death—even death on a cross!

Therefore God exalted him to the highest place and gave him the name that is above every name....

When we are focused on esteeming others and looking out for their interests as well as our own, we all gain, because we are all looking out for each other. It is our servanthood that leads to greatness in the kingdom of God. James 4:10 instructs us:

Humble yourselves before the Lord, and he will lift you up.

I found all that a little confusing to think about. The explosion of interest in our work and ministry was certainly 'lifting us up' in the field of kingdom work, but, when I managed to grab a few moments at my prayer desk, I slowly began to realise that I was actually losing humility before God. 'Look at all these people who are coming!' I would tell myself. 'Aren't we doing well!'

Yet another part of the jigsaw was on its way to me. In truth it was more like a brick being dropped on my head. Never mind building up the work at The Well, I had to find ways of reducing it; I felt, for the first time, a real urge to get the ministry out of there. "But, Lord," I questioned, "that can't be right. Anointed ministries grow and flourish, how come I feel the need to move it out of The Well?"

I often find myself remarking to people these days that I am not paid by the Lord to be successful; I am paid to be obedient. When we stop being obedient, we start faking Christianity.

Obedient to what? In the end the answer, the reason, was more than clear: obedient to him; to his Word—

"Freely you have received, freely give!"

8

MAVIS

Later on that summer, Mavis died. Grief flooded through the team at The Well, but it was tinged with thanksgiving and celebration. Mavis had first come to us as a regular visitor to the Centre for some months, seeking solace from God for the loss of one of her sons, and she began to blossom again, bathed in the love of Christ.

Before long, she began to share her healing quite openly with others who came, telling of the mighty healing acts of him who had gently called her out of the darkness of her grief into his marvellous light. She was a holy lady. It was always a joy to be in her company. If purity is the personal and moral aspect of holiness, and priesthood the sacrificial dimension, Mavis knew that *proclamation* is its evangelistic and prophetic outreach. It became vitally important in her life. She soon joined the team, and opportunities to meet and pray with others became her greatest joy.

Leonard Griffith expressed the significance of proclamation well when he said, 'Outreach, evangelism, and mission are not optional activities like bowling, billiards, and ping-pong for the members of a religious club. They are mandates from Christ himself, part of the original givenness of the gospel.' Holiness is not merely for our own benefit. Mavis demonstrated to me that we are called to be holy for God, who wants us to be light and salt in the world. Because the good news was a living reality to her, she knew she was forgiven and redeemed, released as a Christian from the grip of sin and death and the devil. She was demonstrably a member of Christ's everlasting kingdom. Jesus was her Lord and she was an ambassador for him, and accountable to him. She wanted to bless others through her healing, bubbling at the very thought of it. Through her practical, Christian kingdom living, she set an example that simply could not be ignored.

As the weeks and months went by, Mavis developed cancer which, despite surgery, invaded the inside of her body until she was too weak and too ill to minister any more. During the latter stages of her illness, trips to be with her, at home and in hospital, never turned out the way the visitor expected. As soon as anyone sat down at her bedside, she would ask with enormous grace, "Can I pray for you?"

Christ was in her. Her body was dying because of the cancer, yet her spirit was truly alive because of the righteousness that is Christ's gift. What, through worldly eyes, might have seemed like great darkness, was a shining light to Mavis. Like the early patriarchs, her eyes were up and over her immediate horizon. She knew in the bottom of her soul that this was only the transition stage between her earthly existence and heaven. She was on her way to Jesus, and she proclaimed it. She was on the way to her promised land.

One day, towards the end, I asked her what she was praying about for herself. "God gives us the desires of our hearts!" she informed me in a matter-of-fact sort of way. "So I've been asking him for mine."

"What would that be?"

I confess I was quite surprised by her answer: "I would just love to meet David Essex before I go to heaven!"

Some of us pray for happier marriages or safer homes. Some long for a car that actually works properly, and others pray for financial difficulties to be resolved. Mavis wanted to meet, after Jesus, her second most favourite man!

Three days later, a nurse came into her room and announced, "Mavis, you have a visitor." In walked David Essex!

On the window sill in the kitchen at The Well Centre is a photograph of the singer, sitting with Mavis in the hospital. She had been given a desire of her heart!

At her funeral service, someone read out one of her favourite scriptures, that she had often shared with me in early morning prayers at The Well:

> Your arm is endued with power;
> your hand is strong, your right hand exalted.
> Righteousness and justice are the foundation of your throne;
> love and faithfulness go before you.
> Blessed are those who have learned to acclaim you,
> who walk in the light of your presence, O LORD.
> They rejoice in your name all day long;
> they exult in your righteousness.
>
> *Psalm 89:13–16*

Four nurses from the hospice came to her funeral, so struck by something they could not name. It was as though they had been sunburned by the reflection of Christ in Mavis as she spoke with everyone with her unveiled face.

She had shown me more, much more, about holiness, by reflecting something of the love of Christ; and there were obvious ongoing side effects to this holiness—people around her got healed. I have heard a number of stories, over the years, of folk who came to Christ because they had seen something in others that they wanted for themselves. In Mavis, I glimpsed holiness, and I wanted it, too. In bringing strength to Mavis through her weak places, God had given her a road to renewal through her own brokenness, in her vulnerability, and through healing deep in her life. The holy vulnerability that we caught sight of in her is very close to sanctified brokenness. Holy brokenness is not easy to define, but can be seen quite clearly in the reactions of Jesus as he approached the cross. Supremely, we see it in his crucifixion.

To do the will of God sometimes leads even to our own Christian brothers and sisters not understanding; at such times, we can recall that Jesus' brethren were not entirely faithful at his point of brokenness. Think of Peter's denial! If we can bow our heads, simply continuing to obey God and accepting his will, despite the misunderstandings around us, then we begin to approach this idea of holy brokenness. When we are misrepresented or deliberately misinterpreted, we remember that Jesus was falsely accused, and yet he held his peace. Recalling this, we are released from the need to attempt to justify ourselves. When another person is preferred to us, and we are deliberately passed over, we may remember that the crowd cried, 'Away with this man and release unto us Barabbas.' Jesus knew what it was to be rejected by people. He knows what it is like for us. Sometimes our plans are brushed aside by our leaders, or perhaps we see the work of years brought to dust by what appears to be the ambition of others. We remember that Jesus allowed men to lead him away to crucify him, and he accepted that place of apparent failure. He was not made bitter by the injustice. For Jesus, insults, rejection and the cross just provided more opportunities for love and the release of forgiveness.

When, in order to be in the right place with God in a particular set of circumstances, it is necessary to take the humbling path of confession and restitution, remember that Jesus made himself of no reputation and humbled himself unto death, even death on the cross—then we can bow our heads in this holy brokenness.

When others behave badly towards us, we do well to remember that, when he was crucified, Jesus prayed, 'Father, forgive them, for they know not what they are doing.' This is hard, and can take a lifetime to get to grips with. But if we can then bow our heads and accept any behaviour towards us as being permitted (though not willed) by our loving Father, then this is brokenness. How hard it may be sometimes, but we must apply in our own hearts and minds this scripture:

And we know that in all things God works for the good of those who love him, who have been called according to his purpose.

Romans 8:28

When people expect the impossible of us, and more than time or human strength can give, remember that Jesus said, 'This is my body which is given for you.' If we can repent of our self-indulgence and lack of self-giving to others, then we begin to understand the power of this brokenness. It is not that there is anything romantic or wonderful about being wounded, or experiencing chaos in life. Quite simply, I was now discovering something extraordinarily special about the Christian healing ministry: through brokenness, through experiencing life at the margins of existence, the wounded are brought into the presence of God and discover his love for them. Wounds are painful. They leave scars, which may be dead, tender, hard, beautiful, fascinating, terrifying, pathetic. These scars can easily distort meaning and our perception of reality, and the healing ministry is focused as much on mending meanings as on physical repair. The Holy Spirit comes to mend all, and sometimes, with our scars, we can all rejoice in what they tell us. When we see the healed scars, we are reminded of God's wonderful healing work in us. Then, like countless other faithful Christians who have run the race faithfully, we too can walk behind the living Lord Jesus Christ towards our own death, heads held high in the joy of what is set before us, confident in the hope of a joyful resurrection and eternal life in his loving presence.

9

LAMPSHADES

For several months after the funeral of our friend and colleague, Mavis, the word 'shine' hovered over me like a dove; it would not go away. After the first year of the explosion of interest in The Well, it was stocktaking time. Things were undoubtedly going well, but to coast with the engine idling is to go downhill. God had said "Arise", and things were rising! God had said "Shine", and that could have meant anything I wanted it to.

What does it mean to let our light so shine before others that they will see our good works and give the glory to God? Was The Well Centre merely a 'good work'?

God's undoubted presence at The Well was proving to be a light of healing, and a source of new meaning to broken lives. Was this the light that I should place on a table, so that it lit the whole, or at least some part, of the house of God? I needed to discover what the light of Christ really was. As money burns a hole in a pocket, so this word 'shine' was boiling away in the back of my brain. It had to be dealt with.

Later that spring, a strange thing happened. It was only a small thing, but God has a habit of whispering to us in the lowly places, the times of quiet in our lives. At the end of our time of early prayer, one Monday morning, we had all gathered in the kitchen at The Well Centre, to make coffee. As we stood around, waiting for the kettle to boil, I was nudged, gently at first, by the Holy Spirit. For some reason, the thought had come to me that God can often speak to us in the aftermath of a time of prayer, rather than during it. Two words came to mind: "Go back." Clutching a mug of hot coffee, because the morning was a cold one, I went back to the prayer room and sat down to wait. I was quite expecting to hear from him, perhaps some new revelation of truth, perhaps a word of knowledge for someone coming in for ministry that morning. A quarter of an hour went by in complete silence. There was nothing. After waiting a few moments I prayed, "Sorry, Lord, I must have misunderstood!" —and lost all pretence at concentration from that point on. My mind began to wander around the little ministry room, to the sofa and the other armchair, the curtains that really needed to be replaced with new ones, and the carpet with too many dog hairs on it. I listened a while to the birdsong outside the window, and wondered if we had enough money to have double glazing installed before the winter set in. But then I might not be able to hear the dawn chorus during morning prayers. They are a great lift at the start of a new week, singing in the early light.

In the corner of the room was a lamp, still switched on from the morning's prayer session, and I got stiffly out of my chair to turn it off. As I stood in front of it, God finally began to get through to me.

"We need a new lampshade." At the time, that did not seem a particularly godly saying! It felt as though it was a purely human thought. Were there any lampshades in Scripture? Could I look something up, to check his views on lamps? Then I saw it. There I was, lost in thought, considering this humble lampstand.

Make every effort to live in peace with all men and to be holy; without holiness no one will see the Lord.

Hebrews 12:14

This lamp, like any other, has a base—and a body, which I thought of as representing the human being. At the top there is a light bulb, fully functional but devoid of any power of its own. And yet, this bulb seemed to me that morning to be like our spirit, deep at the centre of our beings. It needs a two-core cable, connecting the whole to the mains supply. I thought of the one core standing for our worship to God and the other as the power supply of his love for us. The lamp has a switch, that we may think of as the baptism of the Holy Spirit, and that switch has on it the hand of Jesus Christ. When we receive Jesus, he makes his home in us; we begin to dwell in him, and he dwells in us. He puts a new Spirit— the Holy Spirit—in us. When we are immersed in the Holy Spirit, the power of God flows freely, and the love of Jesus shines brightly in us. Something of his glory begins to be visible in the life of the person who has within them the light of Christ. But covering the bulb is the lampshade, which hangs there in a complete range of colours and patterns of differing thicknesses, all of which soften, discolour and sometimes obliterate the glow altogether. I thought of the lampshade as being like our sinful nature. The distorting effect—the pattern—was formed as a result of our sins, our reactions towards others and to difficult circumstances as a result of past wounds, our hang-ups, and sometimes our contrary wills.

Jesus has given the healing ministry as a gift to the Church, to help in the deepening of our relationship with the Father and, by the help of the Holy Spirit, to increase the transparency of our 'lampshades'. It is not just about healing diseases; it is about walking humbly with God, and with other Christians, further along the road towards our final salvation.

I sat down in the chair again, waiting for more, overcome by the thought that the Light came to light us; and we are the ones the world sees. If we Christians do not appear to be different from anyone else in the street, then what sort of a witness is that? Without holiness, no one will see the Lord. We are to reflect the glory light which we see in his face—into the darkness, which is what life seems to be to so many people. Not only do those who do not share the

Christian faith have darkness around them, but so also do many Christians who are in trouble of any kind—and that is most of us! Many who live in worldly ways are well used to the dark of the night.

Our God has commanded light to shine in the darkness, and has himself shone in our hearts, to give us the light, to enable us to be a reflection of the face of Jesus Christ. God's light can shine through us, and often it seems that it does so more brightly when we are broken, so that those around us can see his glory, and know that he is real.

We fight so hard to stay whole and unbroken, thinking that, if only our lives were perfect, we could demonstrate the reality of God to others. But our healed brokenness allows God to shine through, and his grace and mercy are revealed for the world to see.

To be walking through life with Christ means a lifelong search for cleansing, for purification from sin, and for polishing our reflective surfaces so that the glory light, the Holy Spirit fruit, our reflection of the personality of Jesus, flows with increasing freedom.

This extract from the Old Testament came to me, confirming these thoughts:

> The sun will no more be your light by day, nor will the brightness of the moon shine on you, for the LORD will be your everlasting light, and your God will be your glory.
>
> Your sun will never set again, and your moon will wane no more; the LORD will be your everlasting light, and your days of sorrow will end.
>
> Then will all your people be righteous and they will possess the land forever. They are the shoot I have planted, the work of my hands, for the display of my splendour.
>
> *Isaiah 60:19*

No wonder I had been so urged by God to discover the nature of light. This was not to be just any old piece of the jigsaw puzzle, it was the centrepiece.

From that point on, I wanted nothing more than to be available, somehow, for the display of his splendour.

St. Paul wrote:

> Now the Lord is the Spirit, and where the Spirit of the Lord is, there is freedom. And we, who with unveiled faces all reflect the Lord's glory, are being transformed into his likeness with ever-increasing glory, which comes from the Lord, who is the Spirit.
>
> *2 Corinthians 3:17–18*

Transformed? I loved the idea of transformation, but was it real? There have been thousands of opportunities to see transformation at The Well. In so many cases, past wounds were being brought into the light of Christ; reactions to past events were being healed. But this is not enough. There must be more; there must be more beyond this work.

At this point in my meditation, I closed my eyes, resolving to spend a little time in worship, in tune with the birdsong filtering through the window. As the word 'worship' crossed my mind, it acted as a sort of bridge to Romans 12:1f,

> Therefore, I urge you, brothers, in view of God's mercy, to offer your bodies as living sacrifices, holy and pleasing to God—this is your spiritual act of worship. Do not conform any longer to the pattern of this world, but be transformed by the renewing of your mind. Then you will be able to test and approve what God's will is—his good, pleasing and perfect will.

Remembering those words released in me a fresh understanding of the real desires of God, and of my own soul; and of the fact that we are designed to come into line with his perfect will.

I wanted to discover God's will for those I pray for. If I really could find out his will for them, and pray into that, then my prayers would always be answered. Would that not be wonderful?

Paul's teaching indicated that I could do this if I got into the business of renewal of the mind. This, of course, can only be achieved by, and with, the healing grace of Jesus. It is certainly not a matter of 'mind over matter'! It meant that I would have to continue to search for, and surrender, any ways of thinking I might have grown up with, which conform to worldly ways of understanding and regarding others.

This kind of surrender was the new 'risk' I was now called to take. I saw that there would be little point in just becoming aware of the things in me that do not look like Jesus unless I was prepared to live in a repentant mode, holding those darker bits to his light and inviting him to come and deal with them. But if I did have the courage to walk this way, God would consider such prayer of surrender as true, spiritual worship.

This thought actually re-defined worship for me. Until then, I had always thought of hymn or chorus singing as worship, but now I saw it as praise. That is something different. True spiritual worship is an act of surrendering to God those little places where, in the natural, we might have believed he would never wish to be. There is a sense in which keeping him out betrays the Pharisee in all of us. It is as though we are almost saying, 'God would have nothing to do with this!'

So what would this sort of life — this pilgrimage road of a 'surrendered life'— do for my relationship with God? According to Paul it would please my heavenly Father. I dare to testify to the truth of this. Staggering, hesitatingly, along the path that Paul begs us all to take, I have sought to grow. How could any minister not wish to do so? In all things, we are to have the 'mind of Christ' that is the gift of God to his faithful people.

Many of us feel uplifted by special services and celebrations! No wonder we 'park' in fine and encouraging times, and then seem to drain away afterwards! The Holy Spirit comes and fills us anew, but we sometimes lose our awareness of his presence, as we drift from the way of holiness and let our friendship with Jesus take a back seat in our lives.

There was a faint whisper behind my ear: "No Parking!" I had to keep moving. Holding the word 'transformation' in my hands, I set off again on my search for true, sacrificial worship and discipleship.

10

SAFARI VIEW

Yet more jigsaw pieces were falling into place. They were, however, dotted about the floor of my mind, not necessarily connecting up with each other. We travelled on.

It was around that time that Ginnie and I approached our twenty-fifth wedding anniversary. This was a cause for great celebration and needed a holiday of a lifetime to crown it. Kenya, and its game reserves, beckoned. We were due to spend the first week travelling around the Masai Mara in a bumpy, game truck with two large holes in the roof to stand up through. The second week was to be a beach holiday in Mombasa. Halfway through our safari came an invitation to join a balloon ride over the bush. The added expense was too much for us to bear, so we lingered around the lodge until our driver arrived, and decided that we could have an extra trip with him. This, we thought, would be second best, but still worth doing.

One hour later and we were at a standstill, hardly able to move the truck for the surrounding herds of wildebeeste. I could not see them of course, being blind, but the sensations were mind blowing. The smell of Africa invaded me. The wood smoke drifted over the Masai village roofs; we heard the noises, smelt the smells, and had an awareness of being surrounded by something that God had created which was vast, untamed by humanity. Of all the wildlife experiences, this was to be my abiding memory of the trip.

The second week was pure luxury. Our ground floor room, beautifully air conditioned, opened up through sliding patio doors to a small lawn and a kidney shaped swimming pool, surrounded by gently wafting palm trees. The small pool was under-lit at night, a fittingly romantic arena for anniversary celebrations. Through the palm trees there was a wide sweep of white sand, and a blue lagoon inside the reef which separated it from the Indian Ocean. We could hardly believe it was real.

Then there was the day when a young man, about twenty-three years old, took us sailing in the lagoon. The little catamaran skimmed over the crystal clear water in the gentle breeze that floated off the sea. The man was bright and cheerful, with a smile that split his face from ear to ear, with a white flash that matched the colour of the sand on the dazzling beach.

"What are your names?" he asked us, as we sped along.

We told him. Then he offered, "My Christian name is Hardcastle!"

At that point, I had to stop and think. We were both startled in a double-take! Had I heard him wrongly? What sort of Christian name was Hardcastle? All the Kenyans that we had met on safari had beautiful names—all from the Bible, as I recall. We had met Peter, Benjamin and Gabriel — but Hardcastle? I tried to get this straightened out.

"What's your tribal name?"

The answer was so strange to the Western ear that it did not help at all.

"Did you say your name was Hardcastle?" I persisted.

"Yes! You see, I'm a Christian! When you become a Christian you get born again." He was determined to explain. "That's like you go back into your mother's womb and come out and start again with a whole new life. It's wonderful!"

"Yes, I know," I readily agreed, "but why Hardcastle?"

"When I got baptised I had to have a new name. New child, new name. So I called myself Hardcastle, after the pastor who brought me to the Lord!"

He was so thrilled to relate the story of his conversion and baptism, and to do so with an openness that was as refreshing as diving into the lagoon. His whole approach was simple, truthful, open and delightful. He simply shone with Jesus. I went to bed that night wishing I could shine like Hardcastle.

One Sunday morning, after our return from Africa, a friend rang and asked if he could take me to a well-established church in the local town, one that neither of us had been to before. Rumour had it that the place was alive and jumping with the Holy Spirit, with a real 'goer' of a pastor— and there was always the possibility of seeing miracles.

Well, I supposed that one needs to keep one's experience fairly broad, so I took up the invitation and off we went. Immediately inside the door, we were greeted by a middle aged lady. As I shook her hand, she pronounced, "Ah! I see that your head is surrounded by black butterflies. You'd better see me after the service for ministry!"

Had I picked something up in Kenya? Were these malaria flies? I suspected that she was imagining something of an even more evil and sinister nature. 'Bless her heart,' I thought, 'she would probably be the last person....'

The week after we had returned from holiday, a man came to The Well, seeking help in dealing with sexual temptation. He came in fear, trembling at the thought of what we might do to him. I tried to inject some calm: "You have no need to be nervous here," I said. "There is no condemnation for those of us who are in Christ Jesus."

"I can't help being afraid of you," he explained. "I went to ask for help before, from the healing ministry."

"How did you get on?"

"They laid me on the floor. Then, one of them sat beside me and the other one sat on my chest. They screamed at me in tongues for about twenty minutes or so, and then pronounced me healed. Nothing is resolved. I'll never go back there again."

After he had gone, I fell to meditating on the words of 1 Corinthians 13. As I thought of them, I began to apply them to my own understanding of the nature of God.

There seemed to be a string of people coming through, telling stories of ministry that was just as horrific. I wondered—why should this be so? Why can we not just love each other? I recalled that, soon after becoming a Christian, I had spoken of the need for love to a Christian friend, explaining to him that if I could love two people with the love of Christ, and they went out and did the same, then the Church would soon be soaked in love. His response had been to tell me how naïve I was. Perhaps he had been right after all. Yet, even then, I had a gut feeling that the finest way we have of witnessing to the wonder of life in the Spirit is by allowing ourselves to reflect more clearly the light and love of Christ Jesus.

> For you were once darkness, but now you are light in the Lord. Live as children of light (for the fruit of the light consists in all goodness, righteousness and truth) and find out what pleases the Lord.
>
> *Ephesians 5:8*

I remembered how much Hardcastle's enthusiasm for his faith had been infectious to me, and then was reassured that my naïve opinion was not wide of the mark. The fact remained, however: the contrast between our young Kenyan friend and episodes which had followed on our return was quite shocking. The gap between his delightful generosity of heart and the overpowering abusiveness of which I had become aware was huge. Of course, I do not mean to suggest that all Kenyan Christianity is like that, nor that all British Christianity might be so shockingly hard. It was the recognition of a stark difference I had observed for myself. Yet another jigsaw piece had been given.

So, what did I have so far? There was a box with a pretty picture on it: a view of a Well Centre in every town in the land. Staring at it was filling me full of reluctance. Other jig-saw pieces showed great empty holes in the ministry of many churches, and some showed unholy ministries that might be more about personal power than love and servanthood. Two pieces did, however, go together: the lampshade and Hardcastle. They were almost the same thing. If my 'lamp-shade' was distorting the light, Hardcastle's transparency would serve as a positive example of how it should be.

Two things now seemed to me to be needed. The Church should be laying down a set of best practice guide-lines for healing ministry. Secondly, someone (I had no idea who) should be developing some sort of umbrella teaching for the Christian healing ministry, that was loving, scriptural, compassionate and effective.

By this time, I knew that I was becoming inwardly criti-cal of the Church in this particular area of ministry. But I knew that God looks deeply into our hearts, and in there, some-where, was a tiny little bit of, "Why can't they do it right, like I do, Lord?"

Then, I remembered a dream that Bishop Ban It Chiu had described to a group of us at Harnhill Centre of Christian Healing. He related that he had had a picture of a person's body. It was in a fairly bad shape. It was full of disease, some of its limbs were only hanging on by a thread and some were rotten with gangrene, but the head was perfect. He added that he felt God was saying to him, "This is my Church and its condition is my responsibility. I am the head, not you." I took the message on board.

I prayed that I might at least be given the four corner pieces to my jigsaw—so often a good place to start fitting things together. The four words given to me were: Author-ity, Holiness, Wisdom and Grace. Filling in the middle of this puzzle had begun to be a tall order!

11

TAKING THE RISK

I kept on hearing the same old echo from that time in Builth Wells: "What we need is a Well Centre in our town!" Sometimes, I wished I could shrug it off, but it would not go away. I was feeling confused. This is the trouble with jigsaws: they contain multitudes of little pieces, all of which have great value in themselves but lack direction and position, unless we can link them together.

Would this just mean more work, finding more time to be available to other people? There was not, as far as I could see, any more time to give away. I was feeling more secure, though. I was beginning to find my feet at the foot of the cross in this life, and felt the more solid for it. Around two years earlier, I had found the resolution to the paradox of going blind and leading a healing centre at the same time. That was not part of this puzzle; it had been another jigsaw, another time. Although it had taken me years to find it, the only place in the whole world where suffering and love come together, and mean the same thing, is the cross of Christ.

To live at the foot of the cross is to live in peace. I had no one to guide me there but the Holy Spirit himself. It was there that he showed me that the flowing interface between

God and me is woundedness—his and mine together. My awareness of my abiding relationship with him is refreshed every morning, and at the heart of it is the cross—the point at which God, in Jesus, became vulnerable and wounded. It is to this point I come, with my brokenness, my sin, my pain and all my failure. As we embrace, the cross turns from being an instrument of death into the tree of my abundant life and healing. As I am reminded of this, I am led into deeper awareness of the resurrection life.

Walking into that degree of intimacy every day with God is to stare at the possibility of danger, pain and total risk—the risk and hurt of being loved to bits even in the darker places. This is the old and much forgotten risk for all of us, which the Church is being called afresh to take.

I found all these thoughts buried somewhere deep inside the wisdom of one sentence written by Oswald Chambers: 'Our battles are first won or lost in the secret places of our will in God's presence, never in full view of the world.'

Now there was a new challenge. If we were to think of a Well in every town, then what *was* a Well anyway? Did it have to be a reproduction of the one we had already set up in South Wales? There were not yet enough pieces for me to see the picture. A Well could be a church ministry team, but it could be somebody's kitchen! It could be an unwanted or disused community hall, but then it could be—and it did not take long to warm to this idea—an individual person.

That became the focus of my prayerful wondering. It is people who are 'Wells'! I suppose that seems obvious now, but it took a little time to see it. But, what would they do? It is not too difficult to imagine what healing centres, or Well Centres, could be doing with their resources—but individuals? I felt a new danger peeking up over the rim of the jigsaw box. Individuals, left alone to be vulnerable to those around them, would see themselves drained and sucked dry by the need. That worried me a great deal. Should I be encouraging them to sit around being available to every soul who shouted for them?

One truth was drifting through to the foreground. Jesus,

our model of a healing minister, whilst remaining divine became human—like us, in everything but sin—and brought new life to others through his complete vulnerability. There is one state which all Christians share. At our re-birth, the divine Lord comes to put a new Spirit within us. Then his will is that our souls will grow more and more into becoming vehicles for the display of his splendour. To allow this divine purpose to be increasingly realised, we have to be trusting and vulnerable, available to him in our inner places. God is not always glorified in what we do, but in what we can be. What we are is the fallout of our worship rather than our activities. Central to the Christian faith is: 'my life for yours'. Yet it is also true to say that if we were to interpret that idea at any Well Centre around the country in a way which might lead to an attitude of *total* availability and vulnerability to those to whom we minister, then we would miss the mechanism through which God really works in his love. The minister who flies past, murmuring something about not having taken a day off for months, or bemoaning the number of funerals to be taken next week, has missed something vital. We are not designed to be *people* driven but *Holy Spirit* driven. A truly effective ministry of healing and wholeness, pastoral care or evangelism could never be manned by people who 'know how to do it', but by folk who know how to get out of the way! Effective ministry is following what Jesus is already doing, and that must surely mean making room for God! Loving others fruitfully, and loving God, are not two separate issues. Fruitful and healing love for others will only ever grow out of our relationship with God.

The more I thought and prayed about it, the more I realised that the depth of our relationship with God was going to be entirely dependent on two things: how much we are prepared to give up to him; and whether we have the will to allow ourselves to receive, both directly from him and through others. Can we take the risk?

Our ministry temptation, if we were not watchful, would be to go on giving out to others at any cost to our own personal resources of time, strength and health, believing that this is required by the example set by Christ. I wondered if longing too much to be in ministry situations might sometimes be a quest for a security of our own making rather than a calling by God. Hard work, and the rewards of being at the centre of attention, can place the minister in a position of 'control', and can seem for a time to give us the comfort of being released from personal fears. Being 'busy for the Lord' can mean avoidance of a necessary growth in self-awareness; an appropriate attention to one's inner life as a Christian.

The balance of looking in and looking out is such a difficult tension to hang on to! I had been taught to look outwards, to accept my faith and carry it into the world. Everything I had been taught in the Church in Renewal said the same thing to me: "Get the message out!" Nobody ever told me to look in as well; indeed, the practice was sometimes even frowned upon.

This, for me, is off-balance. Of course, I wanted to be a 'hose-pipe' for the Lord but it would be silly to ignore the kinks in the pipe—they are the things, not the source of the water, which can restrict the flow.

I kept thinking that as long as I only wanted to give, and resisted the thought of becoming a receiver, I might be betraying a desire to stay in control at all costs, remaining in a position of fear, when I could be spending a greater proportion of my waking hours in the inner freedom of the kingdom of God.

Many Christians who had been coming to The Well, including some in church leadership, seemed to be living in fear most of the time. It easily becomes a natural dwelling place, and an 'acceptable' basis for our daily lives and decision making.

Those who remind us constantly that they are under pressure and over-worked, seemingly in support of successful ministries, deserve our sad and prayerful sympathy, rather than our respect. They are passing by much that God has for them.

In our own walk of discipleship, we need to be aware that whilst many of our rewards and prizes are for the next life, in this one our badge of office is a towel—serving others rather than dominating them.

But why are so many of us so terribly afraid of what might lie inside us, and why are fearless people such a rarity in the Church? I can only suppose it is because we have two opposing forces inside us, fighting away all the time. We desperately want to be intimately loved, but it hurts to receive it! It is a constant battle. Most of us are not so much afraid of the depth of the darkness within, but frightened at the sharpness of the soreness that we know will come when the light floods it.

In this battle, our fears can be as tools in the hand of the one the Bible calls the 'prince of this world', the only one I can think of whose interests would be well served by a shortage of Jesus-like vulnerability in the Church. The Holy Spirit is calling again for risks to be taken, the risk of being vulnerable before the Father at the cross of his Son.

I found a picture of this vulnerability in Jesus, its consequences, and his followers' reaction:

> At that time Jesus said to the crowd, "Am I leading a rebellion, that you have come out with swords and clubs to capture me? Every day I sat in the temple courts teaching, and you did not arrest me. But this has all taken place that the writings of the prophets might be fulfilled." Then all the disciples deserted him and fled.
> *Matthew 26:55f*

It did not take long for me to work out that this fear is the opposite of worship, and that it is the greatest enemy of intimacy. It makes us either cling to each other or run away from each other, but it never creates deep, true and lasting intimacy.

Something holds us reluctant lovers back, and something else drives us on. My Christian pilgrimage must be towards my being more Christ-like. He alone is completely whole and, therefore, free to offer a 'fearless space'. My willingness to become more like him would govern the depth of my 'well'. It is only through deepening intimacy with Jesus that we become transparent to the Spirit within. It is intimacy with God that bleaches the lampshade.

Such an intimacy with God, constantly husbanded by prayer, was beginning to offer me a true home, free from fear of myself. This spiritual experience was showing me something often missed in the Christian life: the absolute necessity of growing in self-knowledge.

In the wrong circumstances, and under the wrong influences, each of us is capable of committing many kinds of sin. Whilst this fact is well-known, the knowledge of its truth does not serve us until we approach the throne of grace with it. Until we are personally aware of the gravity of our sin, we will not be awed by the reality of grace.

I felt a growing need to invite the Holy Spirit to look deeply into my own heart, showing me in personal detail my in-built capabilities for particular sin. It is one thing to say to people who come for prayer, "There is no condemnation for those who are in Christ Jesus!" and another thing to feel the powerful truth of that affirmation of God's word on the matter. But when God is in our life, confession and repentance become the norm—and it has been rightly observed that the devil can gain a foothold in what is kept back.

The certain knowledge that I, too, was capable of doing the things (and falling into the traps) that so many visitors to The Well have done, puts me alongside them at the cross, where there is level ground. Self-knowledge, rather than experience and theological training, is the Christian's seedbed for growth. Without self-knowledge, our ministry to the world is all too easily perceived as self-righteous and condemning—even though this is not what we intend.

I would need to know the peace and acceptance of being in a secure home of intimacy with God, holding my own darkness to his light, so that I could more effectively encourage others to go that way. Self-knowledge helps to show us the reality and depth of the fall of mankind and the persistent effects of sin within each one of us; and the absence of such knowledge leads, very easily, to spiritual arrogance.

Of course, in none of us is the process of sanctification complete. Our Lord manifested complete holiness because he was wholly God as well as fully man. His command to be perfect might lead us to despair, were it not for the work of the Holy Spirit, drawing us towards that perfect love which we see in Jesus, and want to have grow in us. To be told to set out to be what I never could be, to be set an ideal that it seemed I could never come anywhere near, might only plant frustration, leading to a surrender to the status quo. That would stop the journey. If he really is a 'regenerator'—one who can put into all of us his own holiness—then his command begins to make some sort of sense. Holding my trembling heart in my hands, I set off on this life-consuming, healing pilgrimage of sanctification, longing for Jesus to impart more and more of his inheritance into me; allowing him to affect my own fallen (but redeemed) nature. This was never going to be an easy or immediate thing. Sometimes God works remarkable changes in people instantaneously, but this sort of growth calls for patience and perseverance.

Much of our human make up—our mind-sets, patterns of habitual thought, hang-ups, memories, the residual effects of our parenting and schooling—is marked by a tendency to protect what we are, or what we perceive ourselves to be, rather than liberating us to love God and others more easily and freely. So, all too often, we conform to worldly patterns of behaviour and relationship. For many of us, this is at the centre of our problem. We know that God loves us. We know that a knowledge of his love will transform us, making us more like Jesus; but so often there seems to be some sort of barrier, about which we could never speak, between that divine love and our own hearts. We know that the sun is shining but so often, as the song says, 'clouds got in my way'. Somehow, there can be a protective shell around our soft hearts, which makes intimacy with God difficult. Longing to give and re-ceive affection in Jesus with fellow human beings is one sign that God is truly in us, and that we have passed from death into life. Many of us long for a deeper love relationship with God, and for a greater ability to give and receive affection easily with others. As much as I may love to think of the Christian Church as being a family, we are usually very far from having a family-sized open heart towards each other. We simply do not share our lives at the level that God would wish us to within his family, the Body of Christ. It was easy to see that this lack of 'familyness' is often a major stumbling block for newcomers to the Church, new converts, who do not always see in our coolness towards each other the true Light, which is Christ.

How, I wondered, is it possible to die to sin without identifying myself with the crucified Christ? Thomas à Kempis, the fourteenth century monk, wrote in *The Imitation of Christ*: 'Jesus now has many lovers of His Heavenly Kingdom, but few bearers of His cross.'

Too many of us in the Church today want to have Easter without Good Friday. 'All heaven is interested in the cross of Christ, all Hell terribly afraid of it, while men are the only beings who more or less ignore its meaning' —Oswald Chambers.

What is said of our ancient ancestors is true of us. We were born in the image of Adam and we have the stain of original sin on our lives. We are sinners. I longed to find the intimate meeting place with the living Christ, despite the sinful depravity of my own heart. I knew that through such a pilgrimage I would find a diamond in the mud. We ALL stand before him as the human race.

We might think of travelling through life with Christ as being like travelling down a bumpy track in a wooden cart with many wheels. Each of those wheels may, in turn, represent one aspect of our personality, or one set of circumstances in our lives. One of these wheels may have its rim damaged in a pothole or by crashing into some obstacle along the way. That damaged rim may not be noticeable to the traveller for some miles, but it may become immediately apparent if the damage makes the whole cart shake and shudder.

To simply mend the rim is most often not the lasting solution, since many such bumps and bashes will knock the hub of the wheel off-centre. The true 'centre', or 'drive shaft' should of course be in perfect alignment with the will of God. Each damaged wheel should be re-tuned with the drive shaft before the rim is mended, and the cart successfully sets off again. The psalmist wrote:

> Search me, O God, and know my heart;
> test me and know my anxious thoughts.
> See if there is any offensive way in me,
> and lead me in the way everlasting.
>
> *Psalm 139:23*

There are times when my heart, like all our hearts, is filled with anxiety and worry. At such times, we seem to search in vain for any peace. The stresses and struggles of daily living cloud over our souls, and we find ourselves losing sight of God and his plan for our life. When that happens, we find ourselves drawing away from him and retreating inside.

I did not really understand it at the time, but this wilderness experience was about to happen to me. The hardest thing to do in these dry places is to ask God to search our hearts, examine our ways, and cleanse us from any wicked ways that lie inside us. It means being vulnerable and opening ourselves to pain—the pain that comes with growth.

None of us wants to think that there is any wickedness inside us, but Jeremiah 17:9 states that the heart is deceitful and desperately wicked. That is why it is important to open up to God, even in the midst of our pain and confusion. His Spirit reveals the darkness of our souls.

When we see what lies inside us, we can agree with him about it. He has promised to forgive us and to cleanse us from all unrighteousness.

"Where have you laid him?" Jesus asked of Mary, enquiring where she had put the dead Lazarus. Throughout the whole of the renewal movement in the twentieth century, including such revival hot spots as Toronto, the Holy Spirit has been showing a reluctant Church that Jesus requires, and longs for, a relationship with his bride. Now he is calling her ever deeper into himself, with invitations like the one with which he questioned Mary of Bethany. It is as though Jesus were asking us to take him into our places of pain. We are not to sweep them under the carpet; nor to just try and battle through, but to take him to the worst places we have, and show him the real points of agony and despair—our 'tombs'.

We, the reluctant ones, are tempted to say, "But what's the use?" or, "Why should I go around with my heart on my sleeve? What business is it of anyone else?"

I have come to realise something of world-changing importance through my long and struggling voyages in the lonely oceans and jigsaw puzzles of faith. Jesus knows full well that any pain we experience in our passage through life can be joined to his, in a way that will bring us a new revelation of who he is. He heard my prayer, 'Jesus, I feel hurt and let down. I trusted people and they betrayed my trust; they deserted me. Will you feel my pain and remove my cup of suffering? Will you spiritually link my small hurt of being let down to your own enormous pain when you were deserted by everyone....'

Whenever I am honest enough to take advantage of, and respond to, his great gift of fellowship, the Holy Spirit reveals to me more about my Saviour, Jesus Christ, who was let down and deserted, beaten up and tortured to death.

Amazingly, everything that God reveals to me in this way, he wants to reveal in me, and through me, to other folk. Each and every one of us may see Jesus weep firstly for us and then, through us, for others. Not only is this a healing experience for those who accept this offer of a 'wound-to-wound' encounter, it is also one of those life-changing processes which will make me more like Jesus.

Once we see what God is revealing to us, we can be more aware of his grace and love—and his peace that passes all understanding. We can trust him to bring healing and peace into our lives when we allow him to search our hearts: he has promised to lead us in the way everlasting, and he keeps his promises.

My heart leapt for joy as I saw that Jesus stretches out his pierced hands to surround with his love all those who search for him.

12

BLACKOUT

There was by now plenty to work on, enough jigsaw pieces to start juggling around. We came across so many Christians who had a real gut feeling that revival was, and still is, just around the corner, but not yet released.

A feeling was growing, deep in my bones, that the time was coming when God was looking for us to understand a new meaning of the word 'risk'. This time he was calling not for the traditional view of risk but a new one, at least one that would prove to be a new adventure for many in the Church today. The new risk being urged upon us was encapsulated in the idea of daring to recognize and name one's own dark places and to hold them to Christ, asking for his healing grace. This can be dangerous and hurtful stuff: dangerous, because one has to take the consequences of self knowledge, and be prepared to make that journey to Calvary with them in one's hands. This, I felt convinced, would lead to a growing inner transparency to the light (which is Christ). In this way, a greater degree of personal holiness is released. This would shine the light that would be so attractive to searchers after faith. Revival would be triggered by those prepared to lead this form of the repentant life.

The phrase 'being strong in the broken places' refers to the medical fact that the healed crack in a broken bone becomes the strongest part of the bone. I also came to believe that through prayer, meditation and healing it is the healed crack which itself becomes transparent.

Out of that transparent 'break' shines holiness, the evidence of the indwelling of the Holy Spirit.

So, here I was, suspecting that I knew a truth about healing and wholeness, and sitting in The Well with the certain knowledge that healing, in its fullest sense, is given to help show the world the Light of the world. How I longed to find the way to make this better known, and more widely experienced, in the Church. If I could do this, then I might at last be able to serve the Body of Christ and people's real needs. What a thought!

Of course there was still a long way to go, still a journey to take to fill in the gaps and find my answer, but I was so excited! With all that I had learnt, I set out with a will, striding out towards the answer. Then, suddenly, it all started going badly wrong. I hit a brick wall of gigantic proportions. I could not understand the change that came over me. I had walked a long road in my devotional meditations, found a number of pieces for my jigsaw, and was more than content with all that was going on.

Overnight, out of the clear, blue skies of gently rising revelation, came the black cloud. All the joy of the Lord was swamped and drowned by a long, dark night in my soul.

The feeling of emptiness was quite shattering, absolutely depressing and entirely unexpected. For the first time since going into full-time ministry, I found myself somewhere that I had only heard talked about by other people: I was in a desert experience. After a while in that awful place, it was not too difficult to get the drift of this tough and forbidding country. Where there used to be occasional little pools of clarity of vision and direction, there were now lakes of uncertainty to drown in. Instead of the details falling into place, as and when I needed them to, there seemed to be endless reverses. I would organize one thing and the opposite would happen. I set up meetings, and half those invited never arrived. I set dates for things to happen, and they never worked out. Life became a struggle; ministry became hard work. Each setback seemed to be climbing on the back of the one that went before. Prayer became a chore, and the pages of the Bible seemed to have no word to give me any more.

When I used to make a mistake, I could easily admit to being wrong; now, when I made mistakes, I wanted to say, 'It wasn't my fault.'

Whereas before this desert I worked hard and still had some spare time to use, now there was no time for anything. I used to go through problems. Now I just went round them and got nowhere. Before I arrived here, I could sit and listen. Now I seemed to be forever waiting for my time to talk, my time to butt in with my 'superior views'.

It had, up until then, been natural to respect my superiors, and to try to learn something from them. In this wilderness place, I resented them and secretly enjoyed looking for any chink in their armour.

Instead of feeling responsible for leading the work at The Well Centre, I started to think to myself, 'I only work here!' Instead of enjoying the messages that other speakers had for me, I began to compare the greater quality of their speaking to mine. Instead of the thrill of gleaning new thoughts from other writers, I became jealous of their writing skills. I was definitely on the way down.

On top of all this, I found myself struggling more and more to relate to other people, especially those who seemed to 'have it all together' all the time. These difficulties were combining to produce what has been described as 'a gut wrenching sense of empty powerlessness' inside me. My call to ministry felt increasingly thin.

After two or three months of this, I was beginning to wonder if there was ever going to be a way out of what seemed like a dire spiritual quagmire. If I had been enjoying a 'honeymoon' period in the Lord's service, coasting along in the warmth of his glory, our relationship was beginning to look horribly like approaching divorce. God seemed to have 'dis-appeared'—still in control, still in charge, but a long way away from me.

Looking back now at that experience, I can see that serv-ing Jesus is a strange mixture of the mountain top, the valley and the desert. Most of us, myself included, prefer to be on the mountain tops, although we are prepared to plug away in the valleys because that is where much of the action really goes on. But the quicksands of the desert? The wilderness? That is another story altogether. I was miserably unprepared for the anxiety which so quickly sneaked up on me without warning, and so easily threw me into this out-of-the-blue tail spin. 'If you really loved Jesus,' I kept accusing myself, 'you would not fall into troughs like this.'

Things had been going so well, and my jigsaw had been starting to come together—and now this mess. It all seemed so untimely, so unfair, a dead end from which there was no apparent hope of return. Why was I in that place, anyway? Life would have been a little more manageable if I could somehow have located the reasons for my darkness, but this proved well beyond my reach, and beyond the range of my training in the subject of inner healing.

I suppose I could identify some small degree of weari-ness and general tiredness of body, mind and spirit through my journeying, but I had come across this combination be-fore and had managed to handle it without this problem. One day spent loafing around the house with a blank mind normally does the trick!

There were a few inner personal and ministry struggles which disquieted me, but I had coped with that sort of thing before, through the grace of God. Perhaps there were more than the usual quota of difficult problems coming into The Well, but we had been able to handle them adequately, by God's grace, in days gone by. After all, I reasoned, I was called to be in that place, not to be 'successful'.

Perhaps it was a combination of all these things, along with other nameless forces, which can sometimes make any of us vulnerable to depression and drained of spiritual energy. Was this the enemy, who was making my way forward so tough? I have to admit that the idea of Satan bothering to mess up the circumstances around me, in order to foul up my 'great' dreams for the kingdom, struck me as a bit over dramatic. Was the devil really frustrating my feeble little efforts for God?

The thought that this desert time might have been allowed to happen by God, my heavenly Father, never crossed my mind. However I pondered these matters, I clearly remember wondering where God was, in those hard days and long nights: "Where are you? How come you have not yet turned up to rescue me?" Over and over in my mind, through the sleepless hours, tumbled the dreadful thought: had I been kidding myself all along—about my call to ministry, and about the deepening of my relationship with Jesus?

I did discover for certain, and have since seen in the wilderness wanderings of others, that there are no easy answers when we are stifling in the loneliness of our own personal desert. And what a lonely place it was! If others had known my own emptiness of soul and spirit, they would have been alarmed and devastated. They would have been shocked even more if, heaven forbid, the record of all my past errors had been revealed to them. The danger of being exposed seemed to grow on a daily basis. What seemed to make this internal examination even worse was that I was starting to look at my colleagues at The Well Centre, and think that whilst they were worthy of the Lord's calling, I was not; that I was just a passenger. This attitude did not help at all. It only served to heighten further my sense of being apart from everybody. What a muddle!

It got worse. Once I had successfully convinced myself of all my own obvious leadership and ministry disabilities, I could sense that I was beginning to turn on other people. The finger pointing began. 'If only I had been given more support from my family or friends, I would not have been in this mess.' 'If my leaders, those I look up to, had really understood what I was trying to achieve, they would have sensed this pain and come running.' 'If the Church were really touched by the love of Jesus, then such downs would be swept up before they cause so much hurt.' 'Where was the love of Jesus in the Church, to heal this agony?'

I had missed the simple fact that I had not told anyone of my plight! Others around me were not able to help, because I cleverly disguised my inner struggle—so that they had no hint of its magnitude. It is amazing how we can sustain the illusion of control and coping when really we are collapsing inside. At this point there was only one thing left to do—to persevere and keep on hoping. In the very earliest hours of the darkest sleepless night, how eagerly we can wait for the coming of dawn over the horizon. Psalm 130:5–6 is a fine reflection of this sense of having to wait:

> I wait for the LORD, my soul waits,
> and in his word I put my hope.
> My soul waits for the Lord
> more than watchmen wait for the morning,
> more than watchmen wait for the morning.

We search for the faintest, lighter grey creeping over the edge of our world, and as the streaks of lavender and pink light stream, as I remember it, across the sky, our souls rejoice in the dawning of a new day. Anyone who has struggled through one of these long, dark nights knows how earnestly we wait for dawn. The hours stretch ahead, seemingly unending. Everything seems hopeless. Yet, with dawn's arrival, hope blooms and blossoms once again. There was the first chink of light from the new dawn as I listened to my own heart.

> Hear my cry, O God; listen to my prayer.
> From the ends of the earth I call to you,
> I call as my heart grows faint;
> lead me to the rock that is higher than I.
> For you have been my refuge,
> a strong tower against the foe.

Psalm 61:1–3

When our hearts are overwhelmed in any dried-up place, it is easy to forget that God waits for us to turn back towards him. So often we worry, straining and struggling against the weight of a particular problem, looking for solutions in our own strength—and feeling faint of heart. Sometimes the tidal waves that threaten to engulf everything lead us to wake up in the morning and not want to get out of bed until the solution is manifestly obvious to us. It would be so easy to stay there and avoid our problems, but that never solves them.

Thankfully, God does not forget you or me when we look as if we might be drowning. He is our refuge, our shelter, a strong tower from our enemy. When our hearts are overwhelmed, when we feel as if the world is against us, when we feel like giving up because we cannot find the answers, we can always run to God, who is there waiting for us. He is our loving Father, who wraps us in loving arms and comforts us. He protects us from the enemy, and he is our rock when we falter.

The pathway from the desert to the valley, with its green fields and rich, river springs, is a gracious gift of God. I had arrived in the desert for no discernible reason; now I began to find firmer ground to stand on, and greater purpose again, without any obvious explanation for this change. I began to be aware once more of God's love and care for me.

Later, I wrote in my journal, 'Anyone's journey into the heart of God is never without hair-raising encounters with ourselves and the world around us. We may not be able to completely enjoy the air at the mountain peak if we have not gasped for life in the valley of death.'

Try as I might, there had been no way out *in my own strength*. None of us gets to map our own escape routes from these awful wilderness places. I was gently led forwards by God, who has a habit of looking for us in the hard roadsides of life. I had to learn the tough way not to be afraid. His grace is sufficient. My life was being shaped by a new found dependence and trust. This is the refining work found in the desert. There are other lonely souls out there, doing battle. Those of us who have looked grief, depression and despair fair and square in the face, and who, in fearful and tearful moments, have been surprised by God's grace, can help and encourage others to place their faith and hope in him. This is, after all, God who heard the cry of his people in Egypt and delivered them; the One who went to look for Elijah in his own private moment of falling apart, who dusted him down and put him back on his feet again.

I was also learning the hard way that the heavens are not made of stone—our prayers are heard.

Despite my struggles with the Scriptures for what, by then, seemed like a lifetime, I woke one morning in the early spring sunshine to find this extract speaking to my very bones. It was sufficiently full of promise to raise my hopes again:

> Listen! My lover! Look! Here he comes, leaping across the mountains, bounding over the hills. My lover is like a gazelle or a young stag. Look! There he stands behind our wall, gazing through the windows, peering through the lattice.
>
> My lover spoke and said to me, "Arise, my darling, my beautiful one, and come with me. See! The winter is past; the rains are over and gone. Flowers appear on the earth; the season of singing has come, the cooing of doves is heard in our land."
>
> *Song of Songs 2:8–12*

If God was 'gazing through the windows', then so I would be, too. I am not visually aware of the scene across the garden outside the prayer room window, but I stood staring through it nevertheless, allowing the morning sunshine to warm my face and bring through the glass to me what was going on outside. Winter was almost over—that season which seems to take up so much energy, when everything around us is cold and grey, and sometimes, for so many, life seems hopeless. The land we walk through in our winter times is barren, covered with snow and ice. The lonely, damp branches of the leafless trees along the way stand still for months, trying to grasp the empty sky.

It had seemed in my soul that all was dead, and that the cold and wet would never end. My heart had felt that way for too long—frozen and desolate—and I was beginning to seriously wonder if I would ever truly worship again. But just as winter was passing into spring, so the barrenness of my soul was starting to thaw as I was given a renewed awareness of God's love. As if to show me an open gateway, a note was posted to me, within a few days, by an intercessor. She had sent it to many people, but it seemed just for me. It was like a message from God, reminding me of several key truths of which I had been in danger of losing sight. Firstly, there was the truth that I was indeed a child of God, my heavenly Father—just as I am. Secondly, I was reminded that his loving purposes for me were ordained and planned long ago; thirdly, that Jesus is my righteousness; fourthly, that God's love for me is unconditional (unlike worldly love). I was also reminded not to, as it were, try to achieve perfection in order to secure his love; for I already had that love! —and I was given a new assurance of the power in the cross of Jesus Christ as demonstrating that personal, divine love fully and finally.

It was then that the other possibility began to dawn on me—some people go into deserts *before* things happen, not *after* things have somehow gone wrong. Moses spent forty years in one; Joseph spent time in slavery and prison. David lived for a while in a desert—chased around it by Saul. Above all, there was Jesus himself—forty days and nights in the wilderness.

Here was real hope for me. 'Come on,' I told myself. 'Wipe the sand out of your toes, put your sandals back on. It's time to get moving. There is still much to do. Christ is risen—there must be more!'

13

MORE BEYOND

The Strait of Gibraltar is the name given to the narrow body of water which connects the Mediterranean to the Atlantic. The gap between the southernmost part of the Iberian Peninsula and the northern coast of Africa creates this strait. In ancient times, there were two huge rocks, one on either side of it. The Spanish depicted these pillars on their fifteenth century coat of arms and drew scrolls between them. The artist inscribed three Latin words on these scrolls: 'Ne Plus Ultra'—or 'No More Beyond'. This message was written as a clear warning to sailors not to enter the Atlantic Ocean. Then Christopher Columbus set off for the New World and returned to Europe, and the Spanish changed the inscription on their coat of arms. The artist was instructed to remove the word 'Ne' from the scroll. Now the inscription read, 'Plus Ultra'— 'More Beyond'. The Spaniards had learned something I was desperate to get some hold on: there is always more beyond!

From his Roman jail, St. Paul wrote that 'our citizenship is in heaven' (Philippians 3:20). For those of us who follow Jesus, there is always more beyond! Why was I struggling so much to find the way ahead? I thought about it, and I fought over it, and when the answer eventually came it was quite obvious to me. It was not that I could not break through, my problem lay in that I had gone too far, too soon. I began to trawl through the memories of my coming to Christ. There were beautiful times in his presence; and the wonderful fellow-feeling with other Christians. Then there were the 'spiritual parties'. There were prayer groups and lively conferences, meaningful sermons to be heard and joyful praise to be given. The Pentecost life was suiting me just fine. Why, then, after eight years of the thrills of this new world, did I feel slightly unsafe? Why the searching heart? Why the need for depth of soil underfoot where there only appeared to be drifting sand? Lent, that third year at The Well, provided a clue—another piece of the jigsaw puzzle. It was during a time of reflection at my prayer desk, just before Good Friday. Three events lay before my imaginary gaze, appearing in chronological order. They were: crucifixion, resurrection and Pentecost. After my re-birth, I had been collected up by the 'excited ones'; their sheer enjoyment of faith had been infectious. I had been introduced directly into charismatic things, without any teaching on the basics. I had jumped from one place to another, leapfrogging over the essential parts that had made it all possible. I had missed some key points about the cross and the resurrection.

By Easter Sunday I became determined to backtrack: longing to find the way forward by going back; back to the foot of the cross. Here, I was sure, I would begin to grow spiritually and begin to hear properly. Even then, I saw a glimpse of a great truth. Everything flows from learning the patience to sit under the cross of Jesus, because when we are there we see what he sees, the infinite glory and love of the Father. That is where I would find the spring—the source—the healing fountains of God. That is the place to sit, listen and learn. If the grace—and then the power—of God was going to flow from the foot of the cross, then I felt a desperate need to be there all the time. This is one of those life-changing revelations which, I hope, will never leave me. It must surely be the place for every repentant heart. As if to confirm the truth of this fact to me, and to assure me that this was indeed the true nature of healing and 'wholeness', I came across this song by the Welsh songwriter Chris Daniel:

UNBLOCK THE WELLS

Unblock the well, my people
Won't you unblock the well?
Let my kingdom come, Let my will be done
Unblock the well.

The river poured through in 1904
But it disappeared under ground
Could it happen again like it happened before?
Can't you hear my thunder sound?

And water will flow once more from the throne
When my rain falls again on this land
Are the culverts repaired, are the wells overgrown?
This time, will my people stand?

And the river of life will flow again,
and heaven will cast out hell
Jesus your Lord once again will reign
So you must unblock the well.

I know he had not written this song about The Well Centre but, the first few times I heard it, it sounded as if he had! Each occasion I sang, I could hear an earlier message loudly and clearly— "No Parking!"

Not long after this change of route, I heard a story about a young man and an old preacher. The young man had lost his job and did not know which way to turn, so he went to see the old preacher for guidance. Pacing about the preacher's study, the young man ranted and raved about his problem. Finally, he clenched his fist and shouted, "I've begged God to say something to help me. Tell me, sir, why doesn't God answer?" The old preacher, who sat across the room, spoke something in reply, something so hushed that it was inaudible. The young man stepped across the room. "What did you say?" he asked. The preacher repeated himself, but again in a tone as soft as a whisper. So the young man moved closer until he was leaning on the preacher's chair. "Sorry," he said. "I still didn't hear you." With their heads bent together, the old preacher spoke once more.

"God sometimes whispers," he said, "so we will move closer to hear him." This time the young man heard, and understood what the preacher was trying to say.

We all want God's voice to thunder through the air with the answer to our problem. But God often speaks in the still, small voice, the gentle whisper. Perhaps there is a reason for this. Nothing draws our human focus quite as effectively as a whisper. God's 'whisper' means that I must stop my ranting and move close to him, until my head is bent together with his. Then, as I listen, I will hear my answer. Better still, I find myself closer to God. If we are not prepared to be heedful, instead paying little attention to the way the Spirit of God works in us and speaks to us, we will become spiritual hypocrites. We see where other people are failing, and then we take our discernment and turn it into 'prayerful' comments of ridicule and criticism—instead of interceding for them. So that we can minister his love and compassion, God sometimes reveals to us some of the truth about others—not through the sharpness of our minds, but through the direct penetration of his Spirit. If we are not attentive to him, then we will be completely unaware of the source of the discernment he gives. Then we fall into the trap of becoming critical of others, forgetting that God says:

> If anyone sees his brother commit a sin that does not lead to death,
> he should pray and God will give him life.
>
> *1 John 5:16*

We must not spend all our time trying to get *others* right with God before we worship him ourselves. This, I thought, must be one of the greatest dangers in the healing ministry, if not across Church leadership as a whole.

God sometimes gives us the gift of discernment of spirits, and this can mean being shown things that are afflicting other people. When this occurs, we should pray for them in accordance with God's will, in the light of what he has shown us. What a responsibility! That really is an avenue worthy of humble exploration! Finding God's will and then praying into it would get the job done much better than praying for what I wanted. That can be quite a confusing thought, because I do not always know how much of what I want is what God wants, yet I was becoming increasingly confident that moving in the gift of discernment was, for me, an important part of a life of service which would honour him. It seems to flow from 'the mind of Christ', which Paul assures Christians is theirs:

> The spiritual man makes judgements about all things, but he himself is not subject to any man's judgement: "For who has known the mind of the Lord that he may instruct him?" But we have the mind of Christ.
>
> *1 Corinthians 2:15–16*

I began to grasp the point I can be sufficiently transformed by God's grace and mercy for him to get through to me more and more. The indwelling Holy Spirit constantly invites me to listen to the delicate inspirations that gradually affect more and more aspects of our lives when we are open to being changed. It is *his* inspiration that leads us away from expressing the worldly attitudes which are of the old self, the flesh; so that we may manifest instead something of the infinite goodness and tenderness of the Lord. It was true Christian maturity that I had been yearning for: the kind of growth that brings us so close to him that we have *his* mind concerning the people for whom we pray.

By now I had become convinced that my servant future lay in seeing people as God sees them, and then being sensitive enough to pray into his will for them. Not only did I see this as the outworking of maturity, I realised that these were the characteristics that God was growing in those who were learning to be effective in his Church. To grow up in Christ is to grow up in the righteousness which is his gift, given when we receive Jesus; and becoming ever more aware of the personal significance of his death. It could be said to be travelling the way of the cross in the resurrection life. As Paul wrote:

> I want to know Christ and the power of his resurrection and the fellowship of sharing in his sufferings, becoming like him in his death, and so, somehow, to attain to the resurrection from the dead.
>
> Not that I have already obtained all this, or have already been made perfect, but I press on to take hold of that for which Christ Jesus took hold of me.
>
> *Philippians 3:10–12*

Looking back over my life as a Christian disciple, I realised that I had found it too easy to skip over Good Friday and make a rush for Easter morning. I had wanted to get to the good part: the rolled away stone, the new life. I would never dream of playing down the wonder of that morning, but I was starting to recognise that it could mean nothing without the Friday. I somehow began to want to know him in his pains. To stand, wounded, alongside the cross would bring me where I most needed to be—closer to him.

This emerging desire for 'compassion' *with* Jesus had nothing to do with any aspiration to 'earn salvation'. I knew that salvation is a free gift of God, received through faith in the finished work of Jesus Christ on the cross of Calvary. I simply hoped that, in my own suffering, I might be in ever closer fellowship with Jesus and grow in understanding. My life today is very positive and filled with joy, but this is no shallow joy—it is rooted in the pain that Jesus suffered. I could not find true peace until I was able to see, and deeply experience, what Jesus had to undergo on my behalf. I have spent half a lifetime going blind, struggling with all the complicated emotions that attend such things, and fighting to make sense of the goodness of God when physical healing has not been given to me. There turned out to be only one place to spend my life—the foot of the cross. Here, there is enormous freedom. I did not really appreciate this freedom until I realised just what needed to be done to gain it for me. I do not want to wallow in that place, but neither do I want to skip over it too quickly. The truth is that I need to revisit it—time and time again. Seeing the pain of the crucified Saviour helps keep me from being misled in sin; but, more than that, it constantly reminds me that the grace of Jesus is not cheap. I wanted to reflect daily on the price that needed to be paid, not so that I could feel self-pity, because there is none of that left in my life, but simply because I knew that through it I would begin to see just how much we are worth—how far God was willing to go on our behalf.

14

RIVER OF GOD

I had gone up-country to fulfil a longstanding engagement to preach in a tiny rural church, miles from anywhere. Nick and Janey, old friends and leaders in that church, invited me to stay for Sunday lunch. Their dining table would be a good place to lay out my jigsaw pieces and to see if any more light could be shed on the big picture. We talked and talked over mouthfuls of good food, but roast beef and Yorkshire pudding is no foundation for meditation! That sunny afternoon found us strolling through the woods at the back of their house, still chatting around the things of mission while my guide dog, Yates, ran free. He loved it! I could hear the crashing of undergrowth to the left of me, scurrying dog paws across our path ahead, and yet more crashing around on my right.

As we walked along, Yates became more and more adventurous, until the sound of the bells on his play collar almost went out of earshot. Where had he got to? Around the corner and down the slope we went; and there he was—having a marvellous time. He had found the stream.

We stood there on the bank in the warmth of the dappling sunshine, and listened to him splashing his way up and down the river bed, climbing out only to dive back in again. "What's he doing, now?" I asked my two friends.

"Well," said Nick with a laugh, "he's pushing his head completely under the water and picking up stones from the bottom. For some strange reason, he's making a pile of them on the bank, then rushing back into the water to get more!"

"Oh, well," added Janey, "I suppose he's hoping the river will flow more smoothly!"

At last, light dawned. Suddenly, thanks to the activities of a black Labrador, I had more, much more, for the 'jigsaw'. It was then, standing on that river bank and hanging on to Nick's arm, that the adventure began to gain real impetus. This was the first time that my 'vision' cleared sufficiently for me to grasp, in a 'picture', all that I had been learning. An image formed in my mind. The way I began to think of it was this: it seemed that through every born again heart there is, as it were, a new 'opening', which we might imagine as being like a 'hole' or 'tunnel'. It appears at rebirth. Through it flows the river of God. I thought of the stream of his love-mercy as flowing out from under the altar in the holy city and back through time to the present day—in through that entry point in the Christian heart—and out the other side, to others who need the water. At last, I had a picture that, for me, depicted something of the process God uses to reach other people through us. As we are opened to the flow of his river, others are enabled to come to the Father, through Jesus.

While we were standing there with Yates, next to the river, my interior vision had soared away into the heavenlies, and another picture came to mind. I thought to myself, 'If I'd been fifty years younger, I would have made some little boats out of something and sailed them on the river below my feet!' Then I thought of the way God releases his gifts as being rather like the work of a boatbuilder. As soon as we see the person in front of us with the eyes of the Lord—with the mind of Christ—it is as though we have focused something of the outpouring of the river of God, through our own hearts. I thought now of the 'boatbuilder' as being the one who decides what type of ship needs building, producing it, loading it with cargo, and launching it on the river. Our heavenly Father gives us spiritual gifts which are like those boats and their cargo—all given by him, according to his will; downstream come these 'boats' of his 'gifts', into believers' hearts; and his love and goodness flow through one child of his to another. This picture, which now took shape in my mind, helped me to understand a little more about the wonderful mercy-flow of God's river.

What had these reflections to do with Yates in the stream, and his submarine activities? Here is the problem for the disciple. The opening—the 'hole' or 'tunnel' in the human heart—is too small to allow a free-flowing current to enter. Rocks and stones need to be removed to allow a greater stream of goodness. What stones were these? The answer lies somewhere in the deep subject of sin. It becomes a great deal easier to understand what 'sin' is when we stop thinking of it as just something 'not very nice'. It is all that falls short of the Father's will in any situation that confronts us. We see clearly what this means when we look upon Jesus:

> Then Jesus cried out, "When a man believes in me, he does not believe in me only, but in the one who sent me. When he looks at me, he sees the one who sent me. I have come into the world as a light, so that no one who believes in me should stay in darkness.
>
> "As for the person who hears my words but does not keep them, I do not judge him. For I did not come to judge the world, but to save it. There is a judge for the one who rejects me and does not accept my words; that very word which I spoke will condemn him at the last day. For I did not speak of my own accord, but the Father who sent me commanded me what to say and how to say it. I know that his command leads to eternal life. So whatever I say is just what the Father has told me to say."
>
> *John 12:44-50*

That passage confirmed my understanding of the 'river' of God. The rubble in the way consisted of all the things in my heart that do not reflect the character of our heavenly Father. As we learn from the Gospels, when Jesus, who was truly God and man, ministered to men and women, the stream of the Holy Spirit flowed out freely into their lives. The blockages we experience—the sin that comprises the rubble, the rocks in the way of that flow, were not there, of course, in Jesus, who was perfect and sinless. It was Jesus' love and forgiveness that cleared the way in those to whom he ministered. It is the same today: his grace and mercy are removing the small stones and great boulders that block up hearts, as the Holy Spirit opens people up to this divine work. The 'living water' of Jesus flows into our hearts and out from us to others.

In us, Jesus' disciples, the perfect holiness we see in him can be grown towards, but never fully achieved. However, the larger the opening in our own hearts, the easier the flow of the river of God, through us and out to others, would be. By this time, I was convinced. It seemed that **holiness** is the one thing that can enable the Holy Spirit, and all his gifts, to flow through us with ease. Was this a cause for wretchedness? Would I have to spend the rest of my life staring at my own sin and feeling guilty? No; the refining process is all in the hands of God. We need to be **receivers** before we even begin to know how to give at an effective level.

> He [God] will sit as a refiner and purifier of silver....
> *Malachi 3:3*

It was not long after this river bank experience that I heard from a lady who had arranged to pay a visit to a silversmith, to learn more about the process of refining silver. After the smith had described it to her, bearing the Malachi verse in mind, she asked him, "Do you sit down while the work of refining is going on?"

"Oh yes, Madam," answered the silversmith. "I have to sit with my eyes fixed on the furnace. If the time necessary for refining is exceeded in the slightest degree, the silver will be injured. It will be ruined!"

The lady had immediately seen the beauty, and comfort too, in the expression, 'He will sit as a refiner and purifier of silver'. God sometimes allows his children to go into a 'furnace' because he is intent on the work of purifying us; in his wisdom and love, he knows the best method for each of us. Our trials do not come at random, and he will not let us be tested beyond what we can endure. Before she left the silversmith, the lady asked one more question: "When do you know the process is complete?"

"That's quite simple," replied the silversmith. "When I can see my own image in the silver, the refining process is finished."

> Since we have these promises, dear friends, let us purify ourselves from everything that contaminates body and spirit, perfecting holiness out of reverence for God.
>
> *2 Corinthians 7:1*

We drove back to the house in relative quiet. Yates was too sodden to go on the back seat of the car, so he sat between my knees, his head on my lap. My trousers were becoming soaked, but I did not notice. One thing was rattling around inside, one unresolved thought that occupied all my attention. My understanding of the 'opening in the heart' applied to every Christian. It did not discriminate between clergy and lay, male or female, nor between denominations. My picture of those 'boats' of gifts in the lives of Christians began to develop, as I reflected further. As we are swept along in the flow of the river of God, spiritual gifts are received: the gifts described by Paul, in all their wonderful variety, to build up the Church and edify the believer. 'That's all very well, Mike,' I told myself on the way home that evening. 'The widening of the entrance to hearts will bring a greater degree of holiness and grace and, perhaps, greater wisdom. Now you need to consider the fourth corner of the jigsaw puzzle: authority.'

I collapsed onto the garden bench outside the back door, and played with Yates' ears in the dimming light of evening. As I chewed the day over in my mind, I began to examine this problem. It was clear that in and through these 'pictures', God had been speaking to me about personal holiness, and about the use of the gifts of the Holy Spirit in the body of Christ. Now, what about authority? Some weeks previously, I had been studying an earlier form of Christianity. In the far-off days of the early Celtic Church, bishops travelled the length and breadth of Britain, mostly on foot, meeting ordinary people and encouraging them. They sought not only to convert the heathen to Christianity, but also to discover where the Holy Spirit was at work. They provided encouragement, and direction for growth. Leaders and non-leaders alike then visited centres which specialised in their gifting (e.g. evangelism, teaching, healing ministry, etc.) There they were taught by the early Celtic saints, built up into men and women of grace and power, and then sent back to their communities as leaders; they were leaders in their particular field of ministry, and some became leaders in society, guarding the moral and spiritual values of the community. In other words, the Church set out to discover its gifting, then to release it into the world. No wonder the early church was on fire for God!

The arrival of the Church of Rome in Britain began a process of change in the shape of the organisation. Gradually, all spiritual leadership became invested in the clergy; the Church began to operate on the assumption that most gifting lay near the apex of a triangular organisation, rather than being spread around in a more circular shape. To a greater or lesser extent, this assumption remains with us today. What they had discovered, and what we have forgotten, is the way to explore and expand the spiritual life and gifts of the Church—under proper oversight. I was jubilant. The jigsaw was taking shape. And what of Well Centres? Were these all to be like the one in South Wales? It was clear now that I was not being called to create organisations in run-down churches and chapels and other old, decrepit buildings all over the place; I was being called to raise up individual people to *be* Wells. What a beautiful thought that was to me! Ordinary Christians could grow and be built up in grace, wisdom and power. If they could be helped to follow the sacrificial life, on the principle of 'widening the heart opening', then wisdom, grace and holiness would shine out of them. The 'rubble' can be removed, and hearts opened to the free flow of forgiveness, grace and mercy, as Jesus meets each person at their point of need. God had given me a vision which would underpin all that was to follow.

Wherever I could find Christians longing to grow, aching to be finer reflections of the light of Christ, then they could be encouraged to walk this particular road.

There is a longing in people for the reality that only the river of God can bring—the flow of his supernatural power, love, holiness and truth. God is sometimes denied but often it would be more accurate to say that he has been 'displaced' in people's lives. How easy it is for people to allow many things to displace a real relationship with God.

Only the living, active word of God, interpreted by the Holy Spirit, can put this right. Guarding our thoughts is of key significance:

> Above all else, guard your heart....
>
> *Proverbs 4:23a*

Paul wrote,

> Fill your minds with those things that are good.
>
> *Philippians 4:8*

The 'widening' of my heart opening to the flow of God's grace and mercy would require obedience to that biblical command. Each space which Yates had left in the river bottom by his canine excavations would be displaced by a greater flow of water. By the mercy of God, we can make the principle of 'displacement' work for the kingdom! Worries and worldly desires really can be displaced by the love which flows along the river of God.

All must be held in balance. Removing the stones in my own heart was only going to be fruitful if others felt the benefit in some way. The love of God for mankind is *redeeming* love. The Spirit is **truth**, and the Spirit of God is **holy**. Redemption is inconceivable without truth and holiness. The work of the Holy Spirit in sanctifying each believer is **both** to draw that person closer to the Father through Jesus, **and** to extend the kingdom of God by drawing others toward the river of God. Simply, he leads us into the way of truth and holiness so that we can enjoy his presence for eternity and so that others can, too—as we share the love we have experienced. I saw now how vitally important it was that I should teach of his holiness, and about the amazing way he uses us in his work for the salvation of others.

15

KINGDOM WORK

This was the turning moment. This was the time to reach out. I wanted something I hardly dared search for, let alone try to explain to anyone else. I needed to find a way to get our ministry out of The Well.

So many had come to see us because they could not find grace and loving prayer in the local church. Many more had come seeking teaching and encouragement. I had to find some way, God's way, to make known this vision. Could we really build 'Wells' all over the place?

The little team at The Well had grown—and all were moving in grace and truth. Everyone knew, at the bottom of their heart, that the river of God was flowing, and that our responsibility was to let it flow. If the river flowed, the 'boats' would come naturally, and they had started to do just that. No one was 'trying' any more to hear God in ministry situations. *Trying too hard* deafens the spiritual ear, rather than sensitising it. We concentrated our own personal thoughts and meditations on our own closeness to God. We were in the business of 'widening the heart opening'.

We now came to the realization that the greatest gift we could ever give to those who came to The Well was not necessarily the one that the individual person wanted at the time. It might well be that gift, and it often was, but we had discovered a greater truth. The most marvellous thing we could do for anyone was to enable them to come into the presence of God—in ways that were deeper and more healing than they had ever known before. This is what we began to yearn for—not just the specific gifts of knowledge, wisdom or healing, but the gift of being able to bring them into God's presence. In this way, we began to learn not only how to be involved in healing ways but how to get out of the way of the flow of the river. Then our human minds would not interfere with what God wanted to do, and our Lord would have a direct line to every sufferer. Unless we who were ministering were learning to hold our own darkness to his light, that would not happen. We would not know how to show others what we did not practise ourselves! To our amazement, and deep thrill, the gifts began to flow easily and without effort. It was, and still is, a miraculous life!

One visiting clergyman was concerned for us. "This must be very draining," he offered. "You need to make sure you get plenty of days off work, and relax!" Strangely, though, ministry is not draining unless the minister is giving up something inside. We found Christian ministers all over the country doing just that. They were doing the Lord's work for him until they dropped. But this is *kingdom* work; this is different. This is sitting with others and being a simple channel. The water-flow did the work. Spurgeon wrote:

> A job is at your choice; A ministry is at Christ's call. In a job you expect to receive; in a ministry you expect to give. In a job you give something to get something; in a ministry you return something that has already been given to you. A job depends on your abilities; a ministry depends on your availability to God. A job done well brings you praise; a ministry done well brings honor to Christ.

We had discovered something almost by accident; certainly, no one ever taught it to us. We are the opening, but we ourselves are not the river. True ministers of kingdom work are only 'holes between heaven and earth'. How I loved that idea and wanted to be like that! Being a hole is not hard work, though widening it can be a tough job!

The goal of the pilgrimage road to personal holiness is in heaven, not in this world. The journey itself is infectious and magnetic. There is a constant urge to move on. We cannot imagine, for one moment, that we have arrived anywhere. There is always more of God's immense love for the people we meet. The greater the holiness in those who minister, the more others will see the Lord.

At The Well, we found that, in situations of prayer, there are three parties involved—the ministers, the searchers, and God himself. Imagine, for our present purposes, a diagram of that triangle, the corners representing, respectively, the minister, the searcher and God, in a ministry room. Think of the lines between the three points representing the relationships between them. Ministry is actually weakened when the line between the minister and searcher is too thick and strong. We had found at The Well Centre, with great joy, that if we concentrated more on thickening up the line between ourselves and God, then the line between God and the searcher grew thicker 'on its own'! It needs little help from us. There is a tendency to regard *training* as a constant and urgent need, but we now knew that it is the deepening of the minister's relationship with God which is the crucially important factor.

We were ever more aware that we are 'buried with Christ' through 'immersion' into his death—in order that, as Christ was raised from the dead by the Father, we may continue to grow into his likeness. The 'flesh', or sinful nature—all that is opposed to God's best for us—is to be put to death. If we have been united with Jesus in his death, we will certainly also be united with him in his resurrection. In the same way, we wanted more and more to count ourselves dead to sin but alive to God in Christ Jesus.

Two years after that conference in Builth Wells—where we had been given a 'jigsaw box cover picture' suggesting that God wanted a Well in every town—I was back there again. More talks were given, more people were prayed with, and more wonderful worship times attended. I even slept in the same bedroom, in the same lodge, with the same guide dog!

At night, just as before, the rain came sweeping down off the mountains, and seemed to set up a droning sound on the roof. I had gone to bed early one evening, to sharpen up a lecture I was due to give the next morning, when I fell into a sort of daydream. I 'saw' a huge, white mansion, larger than any house I could ever have imagined. A great, thick cloud hung over it. Rain poured down, thundering onto the roof of the house incessantly. The gutters were full, brimming over with water. There may have been windows and doors in the building, but I could not see them. The walls were covered with layer upon layer of vertical drainpipes, designed and put in place to carry the water from the roof to the ground. There were thousands and thousands of them standing there, all ready and prepared to do their duty. As I walked around the building, I found my attention being drawn to the bottom of each drainpipe. Nothing was coming out of them! Sometimes there would be dampness of sorts and, once in a while, one would drip. Around the ones that dripped now and again, there stood a small group of admiring Christians. As I approached, they asked me, "Do you think this is a drip?" Then a more serious one would ask me, "Do you know anywhere that does courses on drips?"

I am far from sure that this was a picture from the Lord, but I am sure of one thing—the message summed up what had been going on inside me for the past two years. The mansion represented the Church of God. His mercy never ceases. It pours endlessly from heaven in gigantic proportions, never waning in its strength and beauty. The people who make up the Christian Church today are the 'drainpipes'— with heads in the clouds and feet on the ground. The particular nature of each drip seemed largely irrelevant to me. My sadness lay in the sheer magnitude of the wasted resource. No wonder! A cross-section of each pipe would reveal the emotional and spiritual versions of rotten apples, old tennis shoes, discarded golf balls and dead leaves and twigs. If only they could be cleaned out, the world would jump for joy!

Would I dare to begin teaching this principle? Would this approach—the releasing of the 'love river' of God, allowing it to flow through our own inner beings and hearts, and all by the grace of Jesus Christ, into others—be understood by the Church? Would the cost of seeking, above all else, to pursue holiness in my own life be too high? I have only walked a short distance down this particular way with God but, by now, everything inside was screaming: 'Teach it!'

The singer/song writer Chris Daniel heard my first, fumbling efforts in a church in south west Wales, and wrote this:

THERE'S NO SHORTAGE OF RAIN

Are we part of the answer?
Lord, we so long to be.
Will your kingdom advance now?
Lord, we're starting to see.

There's no shortage of rain
From heaven to this countryside;
Yet revival to us is denied.
Father we cry,
In our pain and frustration:
Lord, heal this nation.

Lord, are we living a lie, though our hearts have received?
If these wells are still blocked with sin,
The spirit stays locked within.
Love cannot flow to the poor and the lost,
When will we learn the cost?

Jesus talk into my soul
That we must understand:
It's channels we're called to be.
Through us the world will see
The power of your love.

LET HEALING FLOW, LORD

We need healing inside,
To release the flood tide
Of your Spirit you've poured from above.

It's no use asking you to send more of your Spirit's flow
Until this truth we know,
So healing can start.
Do we mean what we say?
Can we live what we pray?
Unblock the well of my heart.

16

'THIN' PEOPLE

The path that Yates and I take to the Centre every morning turns to the right, almost as soon as it goes under the road bridge in the village. It runs up a gentle incline between a grassy verge and some overgrown bushes, then breaks out onto the pavement opposite The Well. As the path emerges, I am overwhelmed by a sense of a change in the 'atmosphere', which grows thicker and deeper as we walk through the front door of The Well. It is a sense of something peaceful and yet gloriously alive! Through the prayers and joy and pain of the people who have worshipped and received ministry at The Well, there is, for me, a sense of the place being full of the scent of the agony of Christ, and of the pain of those who minister—felt whenever the love of Jesus is rejected; and, above all, a 'perfume' of the beauty of Jesus' amazing love for all. Every time I walk into The Well, I wonder if, by love and prayer, we could clear away even more of the cracks and rust that evil has left on the face of this earth. These are the (usually) invisible scars on the faces of those of God's children who visit us. Even more radically, perhaps we could work on ourselves, becoming 'thin' or 'transparent' for God: highly permeable membranes. I am not, of course, talking here about

129

physical thinness! That sense of being somewhere that especially speaks to me of divine love is, of course, all about the special presence of God at a specific moment, and about faith in him. When Moses encountered God at the burning bush, he was told, 'the place where you are standing is holy ground' (Exodus 3:5b). In the new covenant, every Christian believer stands on holy ground at all times, because we are a 'temple of the Holy Spirit'. Under both covenants there is a special sense in which 'the Lord inhabits the praises of his people'. So we are not to have a superstitious attitude to physical locations.

Becoming a 'thin' person sounded relatively simple when I first thought about it, but in fact, it is not easy at all. To start with, our notion of love is often not so much love but self-centred desire; it needs to be stripped down to the bare bones, and then rebuilt. This means our giving God permission to do whatever is necessary for us to become the channels that he wants us to be. That would probably involve being opened and stretched in ways that I still find terribly painful at times. I seldom want to be looked into with too much accuracy! But I knew by now that the flow of God's love through us could change so much if we could only be more willing to open ourselves to the possibility of that change taking place. How deeply attractive this 'being thin' would be to others! Such 'thin' people, do not give off any airs of judgement but, rather, point us to the foot of the cross, where we discover the amazing gift of a share in the holy grace to be found there.

So, I wondered, how could *I* become 'thinner', more 'transparent' so that Jesus' love might be known and felt? How would I approach, let alone share with others, this ideal of becoming a 'thin', or more 'transparent' person?

As if it was to be one of the final pieces in the jigsaw, I heard a sermon by the Archbishop of Wales around that time, in which he mentioned one particular way of looking at the Holy Trinity. He was quoting from John of the Cross, who lived in Spain in the sixteenth century. Reflecting on the life of prayer, he speaks of how God touches us:

The hand that touches us is the Father, the act of touching us is the Son, and the burn is the Holy Spirit.

This 'burn' of the Holy Spirit happens when God, in Jesus, touches us. John of the Cross saw that this process can hurt deeply, but makes us want healing and life even more. We ask to be touched again and again by the Spirit. Then we want more and more of this 'burning' because we know that it brings yet more healing and more life. This is what happens when we are truly deepening in our Christian spirituality.

I knew now that I wanted to be this kind of Christian, bearing the fire of the Holy Spirit: joyful, consumed, on fire for God and filled with the joy of the Risen Lord—yet, in some mysterious sense, still aching and longing for more of what he has to give. That is what 'burning' must be about – and that is our discipleship. This thought went round and around my head for days, like a catchy tune that will not go away. Burn? What was he *really* talking about? What does the Bible tell us about it? This passage came to mind:

For we are God's fellow workers; you are God's field, God's building.

By the grace God has given me, I laid a foundation as an expert builder, and someone else is building on it. But each one should be careful how he builds. For no one can lay any foundation other than the one already laid, which is Jesus Christ. If any man builds on this foundation using gold, silver, costly stones, wood, hay or straw, his work will be shown for what it is, because the Day will bring it to light. It will be revealed with fire, and the fire will test the quality of each man's work. If what he has built survives, he will receive his reward. If it is burned up, he will suffer loss; he himself will be saved, but only as one escaping through the flames.

1 Corinthians 3:9–15

The flames of which Paul writes are from the fire of sanctifying grace. The thought of fiery testing can be an alarming one for those who fear the wrath of God—such an apparent welcome for judgement seems to verge on madness, and it is easy to lose sight of the truth that we are justified by grace through faith!

When John the Baptist said, "You brood of vipers! Who warned you to flee from the coming wrath? Produce fruit in keeping with repentance" (Matthew 3:7,8) he was not being negative. He was encouraging people to face up to the truth about themselves. Of course, he preached the wrath and judgement of God against sin. Such warnings are still needed; the dreadful warning about eternal separation from God has still to be preached—always in love for those who are destroying themselves, calling them to repentance. We do not have the authority to dismiss the warnings of John and, supremely, of Jesus. We are mistaken if we believe that God's wrath is incompatible with his love. It is not. His righteous anger is directed against all that separates us from himself. His concern for us is amazing. He really does care about our sinning—he is angry about it! We are not to think of this divine wrath as mindless rage. He is so persistently serious about our 'knowing joy' that he is intolerant of the ways in which we take apart our lives, and the lives of those who trust us, and try to put them back together again without holding him at the centre.

In our first few years of life as a community of ministers at The Well, from all that we had learned about the human condition, and about God's grace, we had become aware that anything which goes on within us and comes out of us, will be judged in the fullness of time. Happily, sanctification in the 'fire of God' is available today, to begin to cleanse us in advance of judgement day. What a wonderful gift!

John the Baptist saw the fire of God as operating in the ministry of Jesus, who is still gloriously alive and working through his Spirit in the same way.

I baptize you with water for repentance. But after me will come one who is more powerful than I, whose sandals I am not fit to carry. He will baptize you with the Holy Spirit and with fire. His winnowing fork is in his hand, and he will clear his threshing floor, gathering his wheat into the barn and burning up the chaff with unquenchable fire.

Matthew 3:11–12

This fiery cleansing was prophesied long ago.

> Those who are left in Zion, who remain in Jerusalem, will be called holy, all who are recorded among the living in Jerusalem. The Lord will wash away the filth of the women of Zion; he will cleanse the bloodstains from Jerusalem by a spirit of judgement and a spirit of fire.
>
> *Isaiah 4:3–4*

We need the fire of God today—to burn out the chaff in our lives, the sin that blurs the image of God on our 'reflective surfaces'.

Whatever we might want the Church to be, whatever changes we may wish to make, we always have to start with ourselves. Renewal starts with you and me! So does revival. The picture of the bride getting ready for the wedding day is an apt one, which we are to apply to our own readiness for more of God's power and presence. Firstly, I thought, I have to embark on this journey into holiness. The team at The Well Centre would come along the path with me. If I could teach others to do the same under the Church's authority, then we might encourage an army to cry:

> My soul yearns for you in the night; in the morning my spirit longs for you. When your judgements come upon the earth, the people of the world learn righteousness.
>
> *Isaiah 26:9*

There is a wonderful unity and continuity in Scripture, concerning the love of God for his people. I marvelled at the romance in the heart of God:

> Come with me from Lebanon, my bride, come with me from Lebanon. Descend from the crest of Amana, from the top of Senir, the summit of Hermon, from the lions' dens and the mountain haunts of the leopards. You have stolen my heart, my sister, my bride; you have stolen my heart with one glance of your eyes, with one jewel of your necklace. How delightful is your love, my sister, my bride! How much more pleasing is your love than wine, and the fragrance of your perfume than any spice! Your lips drop sweetness as the honeycomb, my bride; milk and honey are under

your tongue. The fragrance of your garments is like that of Lebanon. You are a garden locked up, my sister, my bride; you are a spring enclosed, a sealed fountain.

Song of Songs 4:8–10

And as I reflected on Isaiah 61:10, I began to see what my own response, and the Church's response, should be:

I delight greatly in the LORD; my soul rejoices in my God. For he has clothed me with garments of salvation and arrayed me in a robe of righteousness, as a bridegroom adorns his head like a priest, and as a bride adorns herself with her jewels.

Could I even dare to think that, if we could find the way to expand our ministry throughout the country, The Well might be, as it were, a 'bridesmaid' to the Church, the Bride of Christ? Simply to assume that role would be terribly arrogant, but were we not doing the job anyway? The physical, emotional and spiritual brokenness of those who were coming for ministry was clear to us, and we were seeing the Lord heal them. Is he not already preparing the bride in this way? No one can turn up on the doorstep of a bride-to-be and announce, "I've been a bridesmaid before so I've got lots of experience. I've come to do the same for you!" But we had a growing sense that if the Church were to recognize our calling, things would be very different. Then we could throw our weight into encouraging the saints everywhere to know that Christ-centred ministry changes things.

When we first came to live in South Wales, we bought a house which seemed to grow a little smaller each year as our two sons grew older. In order to make some more elbow room for everyone, we saved up our pennies and built an extension on the back of the house. I confess I was never truly satisfied with it. Both from inside, and especially when looking at it from the garden, it looked exactly what it was—an extension. How I longed to do something to it, anything that would make it look as if the house were bigger than it actually was! Anyone who builds a home extension seeks to design and improve it, internally and externally, so that it grows more and more to be an integral part of the building. The extension is constantly being reconciled with the main building, to make it look as if it is truly part of the whole. So it is with the work that God gives us to do. I saw that The Well, and the ministry flowing from it, needed to be visibly integrated with other things that God was doing in and amongst his people.

A vision for the ministry of healing and wholeness was now growing—at The Well, and in our hearts. It was all about our being drawn towards the state of holiness that God wills for us:

> ...he saved us, not because of righteous things we had done, but because of his mercy. He saved us through the washing of rebirth and renewal by the Holy Spirit, whom he poured out on us generously through Jesus Christ our Saviour, so that, having been justified by his grace, we might become heirs having the hope of eternal life. This is a trustworthy saying. And I want you to stress these things, so that those who have trusted in God may be careful to devote themselves to doing what is good. These things are excellent and profitable for everyone.
>
> *Titus 3:5–8*

Even in the middle of all his suffering and apparent failure, we find the central character in the Book of Job understanding how much God was wanting to return him to the original design. Job wonders:

> If a man dies, will he live again? All the days of my hard service I will wait for my renewal to come. You will call and I will answer you; you will long for the creature your hands have made. Surely then you will count my steps but not keep track of my sin.
>
> *Job 14:14–16*

God longs to bring us to the state for which we were intended—physically, emotionally and spiritually: holy, fit to be his Bride; living in this world, but aware of our true citizenship in heaven.

What about the outward dimension of all this? We were established as a Centre for Christian healing ministry, but what vision did we have for communicating the healing, gospel message to others? Certainly, we were aware of a multitude of different courses and methods, all designed to encourage congregations to become more active in witness—and such initiatives have an extremely important part to play. We, too, would be developing teaching resources as the work developed. But I knew that we must hold on to the insight that the *whole* body of Christ needs to be shining! We were to be available to all who needed us, including those who were not being helped by existing programmes and courses. With such an inclusive mission in mind, I resolved in prayer to teach, not only about his gifts but also his love; and about his amazing grace as well as his supernatural power. Maybe there would be not so much of the 'excitement' which often accompanies renewal and revival ministry, but the reality of the work of the Holy Spirit, who always glorifies Jesus, would be at the heart of it all. Above all, I knew that what I was called to teach was **who the Lord is**. Holiness was to be central for all who were called to share in the work of our growing ministry at The Well.

> The righteous will flourish like a palm tree,
>   they will grow like a cedar of Lebanon;
>   planted in the house of the LORD,
>   they will flourish in the courts of our God.
> They will still bear fruit in old age,
>   they will stay fresh and green,
>   proclaiming, "The LORD is upright;
> he is my Rock, and there is no wickedness in him."
>   *Psalm 92:12–15*

17

THE BIRTH OF AN ORDER

By this time, my enthusiasm for discovering jigsaw solutions was rising up more and more each day. I knew I was poised on the verge of something: the pressure was on; things were on the point of clicking into place.

When my human excitement over some project or other takes control of my heartbeat, how do I know whether it is my own thrilling to new thoughts or something that is really from the Spirit of God? How can I know if I am in his will or mine? Certainly, I want to bring my will into line with his purposes.

It is said that on Arturo Toscanini's eightieth birthday his son, Walter, was asked which of all his wonderful musical achievements his father considered to be his greatest accomplishment.

"For him there can be no such thing," Walter replied. "Whatever he happens to be doing at the moment is the biggest thing in his life—whether it is conducting a symphony or peeling an orange."

What a wonderful enthusiasm for life, and for the things of the moment!

For a Christian, true enthusiasm means being full of

God, who is taking a constant delight in his continuing work of creation.

Even in the middle of other people's pain, it is possible to have holy and enthusiastic joy watching God at work. Even in our own pain for other hurting ones, we can have the desire to pray and praise, rather than have a mountain of despair. Michelle [no real names appear in this chapter] came into the middle of these meandering thoughts to remind me, forcefully, of where this had all started—fifteen years earlier, in the days immediately after my conversion. When I had prayed for our congregation, "Lord, make all these people like me!" there had, fittingly, been no divine response. When I had then prayed, "In that case, Lord, would you open the doors of the church and send in all those who need you as much as I do", his answer was clear and quite pointed:

"If I did that, then you would not be able to handle them." I wonder if Michelle was sent to remind me that if the long-prayed-for revival started tomorrow then we, the Church, would not be able to help the thousands who would come across the gap. Would we have the skills, the understanding, the patience and the love that would be needed? We certainly will not have time for two hour long ministry sessions in healing centres! Would incoming seekers really find the promised healing love in our fellowships?

Mary and another lady from her church had befriended Michelle, a young woman who had moved into their parish, a few years earlier. They brought her to The Well Centre, in the hope that we could help. Michelle was a single mother, in itself not a problem to the local church. Their problem was that she was a considerable handful—she was certainly needy, but demanding, ungrateful, unpleasant, and, according to Mary, as manipulative as a screwdriver. She was one of those people who seem to have a fairly strong sense of 'entitlement'—the world owed her a living, and everyone owed her their support.

Michelle brought with her to The Well Centre her fourth child, Darren. She quite openly informed us that she was thinking of going for number five, despite the fact that, according to Mary, she was making what looked like a fairly sorrowful task of parenting the first four children.

Young Darren was full of curiosity, looking around this place he had never been to before with wide eyes. When they alighted on Yates, he started to say something. Two words only were spoken before his mother snapped, "Do you want a slap in the mouth again? Shut up, or I'll slap you across the face!"

I cried out inside as I felt the shadow moving across little Darren's heart, and thought of the probable long term effects of such verbal abuse. According to Michelle's social worker, the future did not seem to hold too much for her other children either. There were a few good days when the older children managed to get to school, but there were many days when Michelle could not summon up the energy to send them at all. At one point, the social worker was unable to enter the house because of the foul and stale smells that pushed her back from the front door, gasping for air. The children sat, half dressed, in an unheated room, staring at the television. When Michelle needed a short break from her children or an evening out in the pub, she would phone around half a dozen church members and bleat like a sheep entangled in brambles until she got someone to baby-sit.

Mary was at her wit's end, not knowing what to do. She seemed uncertain about Michelle's confession of faith; it might just have given her a point of entry into a family full of caring people who could be useful. Michelle appeared to be quite happy the way she was, and when I tried to ask her about her 'take it or take it' attitude to life, she turned into what I could only suppose was the human equivalent of an angry wolverine.

Watching Darren and his pained reactions to being shouted at, let alone imagining what might be going on at home, would bring pain to anyone who loves.

It is only human to want to mend this sort of family situation. We all have some sort of deep down yearning to help the people we meet, who need our love—or, rather, God's healing grace through us, to enable them to deal with their problems. Many of us, who would think of ourselves as caring Christians, enjoy doing this, especially if it keeps us busy—and not dealing with our own difficulties! It may be that we sometimes forget the teaching of Jesus about having wooden beams in our own eyes, but on the other hand, it may be that we also feel a deep and godly need to mend the lives of other people because their brokenness disturbs us so much. It can be distressing and upsetting to sit with someone who is squirming in pain, or curled up in a ball on the floor, or running hurriedly off the nearest of life's precipices, or in other ways being desperately troubled. It hurts, if we care.

But do we care enough? Michelle's family situation is not uncommon, these days. It may be very far from the lifestyle of well-brought-up Christian folk, but, hopefully, there will be many Darrens in the Church one day. Revival will sweep in the Michelles, too! How will we handle them? How will we display to them the healing light of Christ that really will pour holy salve on their wounds and change their lives?

When they come, and one day I believe that they will, they will not come for our fine sermons or our beautifully dressed priests. They will not come to share in our wonderful traditions or the beauty of liturgy. **They will come to see Jesus because they need him.**

Could Jesus use me to encourage churchpeople to be increasingly effective in ministering such desperately needed grace? I realised that the godly enthusiasm needed could only be aroused by two things. Firstly, there has to be an ideal which takes the imagination by storm; and, secondly, there follows a definite, intelligible plan for putting that ideal into practice. Now I was on the very edge of having both! I was waking up every morning believing that this new day was important, whatever it would bring.

Now I fully knew what I wanted to do. From beginning to end, I had received the message that a Well should be in every town in the country. I knew, too, that a Well can be a person, someone who is determined to lead a sacrificial life in Christ, so that others might be fed by a freer flow of the river of God. I wanted to be part of a particular 'family' within the larger family of the Church of God: those who have the humility to recognise their own brokenness, and are prepared to hold that darkness against his light, at the foot of the cross of Jesus Christ. I did not care one bit whether members of this 'family' were of this or that denomination, nor whether they were steeped in theology. If they had hearts that were open to the Scriptures and to the prompting of the Holy Spirit, then they would be the people for me. Any who could see themselves, in humility, wanting to share an openness to God in Jesus Christ, in spirit and in truth—these were the ones being sought by our heavenly Father, and I wanted to seek them out, too.

I talked on the phone for hours. I rang every clergyman of spiritual stature I could think of at the time, groping for the final piece in the jigsaw puzzle: that piece which would turn this jungle mess of ideas into reality.

I could scarcely contemplate founding yet another fellowship. I did not want to run a 'healing church'. God has enough denominations already—I did not want to offer him another one! Must we have another Christian club, a coming together of like-minded folk who might be dissatisfied with their existing circumstances? Surely not. Yet I wanted some sort of grouping, some recognised body with which I could share the servant wonders of being a 'tunnel' or 'point of entry' into hearts and lives, for the Lord. It would have to be an organisation whose members would still be subject to the authority of the local church and its own leadership. How could I do all this? At last, when my telephone at home was near to melting point, I had my answer: "You will just have to found an Order!"

I knew what an Order was, but the thought of founding one, or persuading someone else to, seemed very daunting. Nonetheless, it seemed to fit the bill exactly. An Order is a grouping of Christians who share a common and particular spirituality, yet stay within the Church and within its recognised structures. The great value of an Order is that it is very far from being just another fellowship; it is formally under the authority and oversight of the Church. It becomes part of the structure itself. So what about an Order of healing and wholeness, with discipleship at its heart? This was getting so exciting that it overwhelmed me, with the sort of thrill one can feel at the start of a bungee jump!

> Then I heard the voice of the Lord saying, "Whom shall I send, and who will go for us?" And I said, "Here am I. Send me!"
>
> *Isaiah 6:8*

Some of the greatest heroes and heroines of the Church down the ages have been missionaries of some kind or other. Only heaven will reveal all the magnificent exploits of these wonderful people. One of those 'earth movers' said, 'I have but one candle of life to burn, and would rather burn it out where people are dying in darkness than in a land which is flooded with lights.' Those were my sentiments exactly. If we were to have an Order, then it would be missionary in essence, carrying the healing gospel to those on the margins of church life. Founding an Order seemed such a high and lofty ideal for a simple servant who only wanted to be obedient, but who was more than a little frightened of what he might unleash. How could a grasshopper like me face up to the giants who would almost certainly be lying in wait along the way? I supposed that I would not be the first person who has been full of trepidation at the prospect of God's will being done. I was reminded of the familiar passage from Numbers:

> Then Caleb silenced the people before Moses and said, "We should go up and take possession of the land, for we can certainly do it." But the men who had gone up with him said, "We can't attack those people; they are stronger than we are."
>
> And they spread among the Israelites a bad report about the land they had explored. They said, "The land we explored devours those living in it. All the people we saw there are of great size. We saw the Nephilim there (the descendants of Anak come from the Nephilim). We seemed like grasshoppers in our own eyes, and we looked the same to them."
>
> *13:30–33*

How often, I wonder, do any of us look at something God has promised us, and quake in our shoes with fear at what appear to be overwhelming obstacles in front of us? So often, instead of seeing God's promises and deliverance in a situation we face, we see the giants of difficulty, and our faith begins to flag. Such giants can take many different shapes. They might be past hurts, fears, people, situations—almost anything. Whenever I see the giants instead of God, my faith wavers, and I face the very real possibility of not merely delaying God's blessing, but losing it altogether because of my concerns and fears. Moses sent one man from each of the twelve tribes to investigate the Promised Land, and when they got back, ten of them could only think of having seen the giants. They had forgotten something important about the nature of God, and what he had promised them. It was only Joshua and Caleb who stood their ground in faith, knowing that with God on their side everything was possible. The Israelites, when they heard these frightening reports about giants, cried out in their trembling fear. They wanted to choose a new leader and go back to Egypt, to their bondage. The way I was feeling at that particular moment, I would happily have gone with them! But, I had to forcefully remind myself, God had delivered them from slavery, parted the Red Sea for them, provided manna from heaven and water from a rock.

"Whatever you do, Mike," I was ordering myself, "don't let the giants draw your eyes off the glory of Christ!" So, taking a deep breath, I chose to look beyond those giants to the saving, delivering power of our Lord, who is able to do all things. He who has promised is faithful, and will complete it! Having now received the vision—which had worked its way up to the surface as the jigsaw had come together—I now needed to do some down-to-earth planning! There are times like this, when I get so excited and caught up with plans, that I fail to remember always that it is the Lord who gives us both plans and the means to step out in faith and see them fulfilled. But he never forgets us! Plans can easily take on a life of their own, and I can get so involved in them that I have sometimes been guilty of forgetting to look to God to see what he wants me to do. When I am not focused on God with my planning, like most people, I react with panic and stress, running around frantically, trying to put everything back together whenever an idea of mine looks as if it might be slipping off the rails. Yet again, I have to remind myself that the next time my plans look less than solid and seem to fall apart, I am not to panic but to stop, and take a deep breath. How much those in leadership need to rest in the divine assurance of his love! As we set out with fresh steps on a new journey into the everlasting flow of his purposes, he will never leave us nor forsake us; his plans for our lives will bring us greater fulfilment than we can possibly imagine! In stepping out with him we rejoice, because the steps of a righteous man are ordered by God.

Relaxing into this wonderful assurance, I managed to find a calm moment and sat down to draw up a list of people that I knew of, or had met at some time, who were Christian leaders of great spiritual stature in the healing ministry, or at least leaders who were known as holy searchers for the heart of God. There were nine on my list. It was not an easy thing for a small person to phone big people with a novel idea and invite them to The Well Centre, all at the same time—to hear a strange vision! With all my courage in one hand and the telephone in the other, I set about the business of sharing the dream.

They all came, every one of them. We prayed, and I explained the vision. I told them that I wanted Wells all over the country. I did not know if that would mean using more run-down chapels, or people's homes, or parish centres or the like. I wanted to leave that to the Lord to organise. I wanted to try and find, with the blessing of the Church, the right people, wherever they lived, and help them, teach them, uphold them and encourage them. Clergy, counsellors, house-wives, factory workers—it was their hearts I wanted to share with, nothing else! I got very excited all over again. I showed them a basic Constitution for a Leadership Board, explaining that I did not want this whole thing to hang on one name. I still do not know whether that sentiment came from wisdom or fear! I suggested to them that, in order to maintain the accountability of the Order, this Leadership Board would have to appoint, and make regular reports to, an overseer. We decided to ask Bishop (now Archbishop) Rowan Williams to exercise that oversight as I was one of his diocesan clergy and, therefore, under his authority anyway. We also agreed that the Leadership Board should consist of a minimum of seven people, at least three of whom would be ordained ministers. No candidate for selection to the Leadership Board, or to the Order's membership, would be excluded on the grounds of gender, race or Christian denomination.

We talked of many things. It seems so amazing to me now that such a valuable thing was opened up to us by God. The healing ministry has always been part of church life, although at times a minor part. Now that the Church has been dwindling in numbers—at least in Western countries—ministry in the power of the Holy Spirit is beginning to get a look-in again. Interest is on the increase. For many reasons, there is a new openness to the supernatural power of God. Charismatic renewal, which has grown so markedly in our own times, has sometimes left the impression that God's healing mercy is limited to something that might be received during the occasional worship service or conference event; but now things are changing. God has been showing many of us the full depth of the brokenness of modern society and its ghastly effects on children—and the grown-ups, too. Now we have the opportunity of raising the ministry again in the public eye, and what is more, putting an ever widening and deepening ministry under the authority of the Church. This, I found quite 'mind blowing'. Would I ever be worthy to set the tone?

Wonderfully, the group appointed themselves to be the Leadership Board of the Order, and elected me to be its Leader. I can only say that I sat there, gasping at the goodness of God!

One thing remained. I had to take this idea to my bishop and, somehow, obtain his permission to do this work.

An appointment duly arranged, I made the familiar journey to his house, and collapsed into the friendly arms of his rocking chair. As usual, his secretary brought in a plate of biscuits, and Yates lay quietly on the floor, keeping a watchful eye on them.

"I want to found an Order!" I thought that coming straight out with it might be the best approach. In the space of ten minutes, I told him everything. I shared with him my journey to find the heart of God and my struggles along the road of personal holiness. I told him that, through that journeying, people were being healed. This was not necessarily a question of getting better from illness, though it often is, just a beautiful movement towards that peace which passes understanding. I explained how we did it—by bringing people to the cross.

"I want to show others," I went on, blurting away in my enthusiasm. "The people in the Church *so* need the love of God to make their lives more sweet! If I can teach 'tunnel widening' under the Church's authority, then I believe the grace and power of God can really start to make a difference!"

Remembering that interview is slightly embarrassing nowadays, as it seemed to be filled by my boyish and enthusiastic outbursts on the subject of personal holiness, and how 'tunnel widening' could strengthen any ministry, not just one of healing and wholeness. Grace before power—that was to be the watchword. I wish I could have seen the bishop's face; I am sure it would have been covered with a loving and fatherly smile! I waited. I wondered. What would he say? Would he come out with some statesman-like statement which ruled it all out?

To write that he nearly fell off his chair with excitement is only a small exaggeration. He was thrilled. Then there came the question of what we should call the Order. We talked about various scriptures that lay on our hearts, and I offered the story of the woman at the well in John 4. Jesus had found somewhere comfortable to rest. A woman came by, involved in her daily business. She and Jesus talked about private things, and he listened to her with great grace. He healed her relationship with God through himself, and, in response, she went away and brought back a whole village.

"Not bad for one ministry session!" I joked with the bishop.

"That's the story of Jacob's Well," he added, "so that's what we'll call it— 'The Order of Jacob's Well'."

This extract from my journal explains my feelings, back at home that evening:

October 2nd, 1997
After a short meeting with the bishop this morning, he gave me his blessing to set up a new religious Order, to be called 'The Order of Jacob's Well'.

I am now lost as to how to go about doing that, though I believe this must be an extension of what God is already doing at The Well. I pray that friends will come alongside the vision, not just to intercede, so that we know something of what God is saying, but also to brainstorm out all the pitfalls, details and possibilities. Who knows where we go from here?

There are some decisions I can make that it's alright for me to make and there are some decisions which I can make but really should not contemplate on my own. There are also decisions that have to be made that I just cannot take, because I do not know the answers. I will only worry if I believe I'm in control, and I am obviously not—so why worry?

One thing seems for sure, one thing rings true although my heart wonders at all the effort that might have to go into this thing before the rewards come to other people. In the beginning of the Book of Acts they were together praying in the upper room. Then the Lord came in what looked like tongues of fire, and then they spoke with great effect. In summary: they prayed for hours, spoke for five minutes and three thousand people were saved. How easy it would be for me to pray for five minutes, speak for hours, and see three people come nearer to God!

Setting out on this freshly laid out path with the Lord, I became aware that on either side of the track are two mighty ditches, waiting to entrap the unwary traveller. On the left is the pit of self pity and on the right is the pit of self presumption. There might well be disappointments on the way which could form a slip road down into self pity and there will be high excitements on the road, too, which might trap me into believing, if only for a moment, that I am really in charge: the trap of self presumption. This prayer of acclaim, this little litany, I felt might help to hold me on the centre line:

> The Holy Spirit has ordained my present circumstances to remove the wrong and to impart the right and to give me a willing heart towards him. To form Christ in me in character and in conduct that the world may know of the Father's love.

At three o'clock in the afternoon, on Friday April 24th, 1998, at Holy Trinity Church in Pontnewydd, South Wales, the Inaugural Service took place. After a wonderful time of worship, in a packed church, the Bishop of Monmouth, later to become the Archbishop of Wales, read this statement:

> We give thanks to God that He calls and equips His children to minister in His name. Some are called and empowered to minister in special ways under the authority of the Church of God. By the gifting and authority that God gives to His Church, we inaugurate this Order, known as the Order of Jacob's Well, to be an instrument of ministry in the Church. Our Lord Jesus Christ called us to go out, teach the Kingdom of God and heal the sick. Those who have been called to serve in oversight of the Order, we commission you to seek out those who express a calling to the Christian healing ministry, to test that calling and to encourage, teach and uphold them in your prayers. You are to seek out those whose lives are centred on Christ, having hospitable hearts that are open to the Bible and to the prompting of the Holy Spirit, encouraging those gifts and ensuring through your teaching that the maintenance of their discipleship is of the utmost importance. May all that you do strengthen the Body of Christ and may all your work be to the glory of God and His Son, our Lord Jesus Christ. Amen.

I do not remember the rest of the service; I cried all the way through it. It was done, the jigsaw was complete.

18

PILGRIMS AT THE CROSS

This Puritan's Prayer of 1620 reflects all my thoughts and feelings on this new family within a family—The Order of Jacob's Well.

> Lord, high and holy,
> meek and lowly
> Thou hast brought me to the valley of vision
> where I live in the heights with Thee....
> Hemmed in by the mountains of sin,
> I yet see Thy glory.
> Let me learn by paradox
> that the way down is the way up
> that to be lowly is to be high
> that the broken heart is the healed heart
> that the contrite spirit is the rejoicing spirit
> that the repenting soul is the victorious soul
> that to have nothing is to possess all
> that to bear the cross is to wear the crown
> that to give is to receive
> that the valley is the place of clearest vision.
> Lord, in the day time stars can be seen from deepest wells,
> and the deeper the wells, the brighter Thy stars shine.

We had done it; we had assembled the jigsaw!

We designed and developed a method of testing the calling of potential applicants, requiring of them the commitment of time and study.

Then I was left with one problem which I had no idea how to resolve. The Archbishop had called us to 'seek out', to get out there and find those who were expressing a calling to this kingdom work, and who needed the Church's encouragement, oversight and edification. How was I ever going to do that? Travelling around the country is not so very easy for a blind man with only a dog to guide him and, anyway, no one was asking me to! I need not have worried—God's hand was moving on that one, too. People came looking for us: beautiful people, with hearts set on the Lord—half healed ones, and half broken ones; those who longed to teach, and those who longed to hear.

People from many places around the UK have been licensed into the Order—lay and clergy, men and women—and so many have been in the process of having their calling tested that a waiting list has proved to be necessary. We have founded a number of Wells, with more in development. God was honouring our feeble efforts to serve him and his dearly beloved children.

One day, a lady came to The Well because she was providing transport for a friend who had come for ministry. During her waiting time she had little to do but sit in front of the large, wooden cross in the conference room, and listen to the quiet worship music. The room has a very special atmosphere about it. It is a sacred place—not through anything we have done, but by the grace of God. Many who come into the room remark on the peace that hangs gently in the air. The tangible presence of God fills the place. Many who do not profess a particularly spiritual life remark on the peace that they experience as they enter the room. As the two ladies were leaving, in the hustle and bustle of finding coats and umbrellas, the driver poked her head around the office door, and said, "Who had the idea of writing words on the cross?"

We stared at each other, wondering who had had the

effrontery to deface the central symbol of our ministry. Who had spoiled the main symbol of the whole Christian faith? Who had perpetrated this act of vandalism? We rushed out of the office to inspect the damage. The name of Jesus was now clearly visible on the cross-beam—where nothing had been written before.

As soon as the visitors had left, and the front door had closed behind them, I called the team together in front of the cross, and asked them what they saw. To some, the name appeared obviously and immediately. To others, the cross-beam was just a piece of wood. Then, as they stood and gazed up at it, the Lord's name was clearly revealed to them. Not being able to see it myself, I began to doubt. What were they looking at? Perhaps this was auto-suggestion, but then no one had told us the word or words that the lady had seen. This was my own team, deeply Christian and trustworthy people, with plenty of common sense. Could they all just be imagining the same thing—at the same time? Fleetingly, I asked myself whether it was April 1st; but it was not.

My mind was racing now. Who had had access to the cross? I made a quick mental note of the two or three people who had taken it down for various reasons over the last twelve months, and came back to the present. Then, as the little group stared in amazement, the title 'Christ' appeared. Then more godly words became visible. What on earth was happening?

The feelings that ran through each one of us were the same. We felt like lowly clerks who had been called in to see the managing director, and who wondered whether they were about to be promoted beyond their wildest dreams, while half thinking that nothing at all was about to happen!

We stood in silence before the cross for half an hour, each of us lost in our own thoughts. Then individuals began to kneel, and some started to weep. Some lay face down on the floor and some sat down, lacking the strength to stand.

These were not superstitious people. My old protestant mind is not conditioned to such things! I have heard reports of statues in Italy that, allegedly, weep blood, but what could this be? The following day, I made contact with those who had handled our cross over the previous months. Had anyone written on it? They all assured me they had not. Had anyone stuck a paper message to it while carrying it around the town on Good Friday? I was half wondering if the rain might have dissolved the ink onto the woodwork. Again, there was no evidence of this. Anyway, it had not rained that Friday. Could it be that we were just wrongly interpreting some swirls in the wood grain? God is the creator of all things, but he does not grow trees with his name embedded through them like seaside rock.

When the cross had first been carried into The Well, it had been an unstained piece of raw timber. I phoned the man who had stained it for me, and asked him whether he had painted any words on it. In answer to his questions as to the nature of the words, I mentioned the Lord's name. His reaction was to break down and cry. If he had painted the words on the bare wood, and then stained over the words, they would appear darker because of the two layers of stain. I rushed back to The Well, and asked:

"Are the words darker than the surrounding wood?"

"No," everyone said. "The words are lighter."

Since then, they have sometimes been darker, sometimes lighter. The words have changed, too. What one person sees is not usually the same as what the friend standing next to them sees. There seemed only one possibility left. Someone could actually have written the words in some way. Three independent visits soon followed, by respected Anglican clergymen whom I knew to be blessed with a deep spiritual life and plenty of common sense. They visited us separately, but each one came to the same conclusion. They looked at the cross and studied it. They viewed it with the lights on, and off—so that the only illumination was the daylight through the windows. All three men looked at the crossbeam from one side and from the other. They stood at a distance and examined it from close-range. One thing they all agreed upon: the words were not man-made. No one has found a rational explanation. If it were not the natural grain formation of the timber, then there were not many explanations left. I asked the men the same question that I had asked my team: "What do you think it is?" The only conclusion that made any sense at all was that, somehow, God had caused the precious name of his son to appear there, like a signature. Was this a sign, a miracle? Was the Lord 'signing' The Well? Was he demonstrably putting his name to the Order? Perhaps we shall never know for certain, this side of heaven.

I cannot stand and gaze at it, but I can stand beneath it and wonder, and it is in those times that I am allowed to feel a little something of the awe recorded in Isaiah 6:1–5.

> In the year that King Uzziah died, I saw the Lord seated on a throne, high and exalted, and the train of his robe filled the temple. Above him were seraphs, each with six wings: With two wings they covered their faces, with two they covered their feet, and with two they were flying. And they were calling to one another:

> "Holy, holy, holy is the LORD Almighty;
>   the whole earth is full of his glory."

> At the sound of their voices the doorposts and thresholds shook and the temple was filled with smoke.
> "Woe to me!" I cried. "I am ruined! For I am a man of unclean lips, and I live among a people of unclean lips, and my eyes have seen the King, the LORD Almighty."

Since then, many have found the foot of that cross to be a place of healing, in the widest sense. Many more have walked past it without noticing it. Those who have 'jumped in to check it out' have often been disappointed. Those who have stood in the peace and looked up at it, wondering at the majesty of the sacrifice and resurrection that the cross signifies, have been especially aware of the presence of God around them. That presence has become a reality for so many. There is no rational explanation for all this. There is only the living God.

> May I never boast except in the cross of our Lord Jesus Christ, through which the world has been crucified to me, and I to the world.
>
> *Galatians 6:14*

Paul, the ex-Pharisee, knew only too well how men and women want their little boast, their stockpile of merit, their recognition. But he came to regard such things, which he had valued before his conversion, as having been no better than a heap of rubbish. His only boast was the Lord.

When we find that we are not proud of our own service to God, but, rather, delighting in him, praising him, thanking him and enjoying being in his presence—then we shall really have begun to do the thing for which we were all given birth.

This particular pilgrimage has lasted for seven years. At the start of it all was the tentative opening of The Well Centre, Cwmbran, as a place of prayer for those who feel the need for God's help in their lives. At its close, God has drawn together a fast growing group of Christians who are being 'enlarged' and 'unblocked', as 'wells' in their own communities.

Along this pilgrimage road, I have found so much of the grace of Jesus, who came to offer abundant life. I discovered that Well Centres were not buildings after all, but individuals becoming more transparent to the light which is Jesus within.

Will you join me, and all who are looking to Jesus, in this pilgrimage walk? He invites everyone, but the choice as to whether to accept that invitation is yours, personally. His love for you is infinite. We have different callings, but as we have seen time and again, no one is beyond the grace, love, and healing power of Jesus Christ, who is always faithful to his promises, set out in the New Testament. Christians are forgiven sinners, and we need to look daily to the Holy Spirit for a fresh supply of grace and power. There is a great urgency about this invitation. Do not put off until tomorrow what God calls you to do today. The time is now! The river of God is flowing; grace is at work; the message of the cross is effective now. All who come to the foot of that cross, in penitence and faith, find the open arms of the risen Lord ready to welcome them. To him be the glory. If your need is for healing, do not be afraid to ask him. He has the power to heal, and is ready to release that healing in your life. Healing, whether of body or mind, accompanies the preaching of the good news. But remember that the greatest healing of all is salvation to eternal life, the forgiveness of sins and reconciliation with God through Jesus Christ.

Let healing flow, Lord!

By the same author:

TRUST YATES!
Stories of a Guide Dog with a Dog Collar

Foreword by Adrian Plass

Close your eyes and imagine allowing a dog to guide you safely wherever you go—then you get an idea of the sort of trust that Mike Endicott and many other blind people have to learn.

Yates is a very special guide dog—sensitive, intelligent and greatly loved by people to whom his owner ministers.

In this book, Mike tells of some of the profound truths he has learnt during his time with Yates.

ISBN 1901949087

UK £5.99 $14.95 in Canada